G000081767

Hannah Imogen Jones MA, BA (Hons)

# Heaven Is In Here.

## One Soul's Steps In Poetry And Photography

Need Expression Publications

Published by Need Expression Publications

Elfed House, Oak Tree Court,
Mulberry Drive, Cardiff Gate Business Park,
Cardiff, Wales, UK, CF23 8RS

The website address for this publication is www.heavenisinhere.com

This limited First Edition print run of 10,000 copies, published October 2012
by Need Expression Limited trading as Need Expression Publications.



A catalogue for this book is available from the British Library.

ISBN 978-0-9570829-0-8

Printed and bound in the United Kingdom
by T.J. International Ltd., Cornwall, UK.

## FOREWORD

Thank you so much for your presence. This is a gift from my heart to yours.
In poetry and photography, I share with you my journey on this beautiful planet of ours - and invite you to join me along the way. Allow these words and images to uplift and inspire you; provide comfort, support, insight and understanding. Allow them to evoke you to think, feel, believe, imagine, dream and fly. I share with you my love, my life and my lessons - the testing times, the trials and tribulations, the joys, the discoveries and wonderful epiphanies that we all experience in our own uniquely amazing ways, on this magical, challenging and beautiful journey we call life and being human.

My gift to you is simple - It is a gift of pure love.

My wish for you is simple - May you find your Heaven.

*Hannah*

CONTENTS

CONTENTS

CONTENTS

CONTENTS

## A BEDTIME SONG FOR THE PARENTS AND CHILDREN OF CAERPHILLY

We live on the aged land of giants
Who stood majestic and defiant
Who fought the princes and the beasts
Consumed the villagers for feasts
They strode the land with massive strides
They saw a child and opened wide…
Some say the mighty things still roam
At night while we sleep in our homes
So please, dear children, don't you shout
In case the giants venture out.

We live betwixt the hills of dragons
Sitting tight in hidden caverns
Dragons older than the hills
Watching closely jewelled spoils
Guarding jealously their treasure
Eating goats and breathing fire…
Some say that if you venture near
Then you will turn to stone with fear
So please, my love, don't run away
In case you don't come home next day.

We live in a place of ghouls and ghosts
Competing who can scare us most
They swirl around the town at night
They hide in shadows planning frights
They lurk around the streets and park
And always surface after dark…
Some say the ghosts can hear you cry
And come to hover at your side
So please, my child, don't shed a tear
In case you bring the ghoulies here.

Relax, dear Mother, please don't fear
I don't mind having giants here
Some giants really aren't so bad –
To meet a nice one I'd be glad
For he could tell me of the sights
He witnesses from such a height!
And if a bad one did appear
Then I would just defeat him here
I have a stone, I have a sling
And I would put an end to him!

And darling Mother, don't you fuss
The dragons will not bother us
They're just doing their very best
To make sure that their treasure rests
And if I ever play away
I will not with a dragon play!
I'll simply hide behind a tree
I'll watch him, but he won't see me
And if he comes out from his cave –
Don't worry Mum, your child is brave!

And as for ghosts and ghouls and stuff
I think they just pretend they're tough –
They plan their schemes because they're bored
Of these poor things I'll not be scared!
And ghosts as well are not all bad –
Some are lonely, kind or sad…
But if a bad ghost comes this way
Don't worry Mum, I'll save the day!
I'll hide right here beneath my sheet
And make him jump right off his feet!

## A BUNCH OF DAFFODILS

This Valentine's day
Sweet Cariad of mine
I give you a bunch of daffodils.
They smell so divine
They're just heavenly fine
They'll look lovely up there on the window-sill.
And don't you agree
That to cough up the fee
For a bunch of red roses is hefty?
These aren't quite the price
But they're equally nice
And honey – we have to be thrifty.

And if I'm really honest about it...
Those deep yellow blooms
Remind me of you
So golden and glowing and swaying.
They dance in the sun
And each beautiful one
Nods as if gentle prayers she is saying.
She comes from the land
Though her trumpet is grand
And she holds her sweet head up with dignity.
She humbly stands
But upon the command
She stands out from the crowd like she's royalty.
She shines in the night
With that strong yellow light –
It's as if her sweet aura is glowing.
And she shines in the day
At whatever you say –
She just can't stop her sweet soul from showing.

So my Darling,
I give you this beautiful bunch
As we sit down to feast
At our Valentine's lunch
And I know you'll agree
That this gesture from me
Is nothing but love
When it comes to the crunch.
And Cariad, I know you will pardon
That they're picked from the edge of the garden.

## A CHRISTMAS WISH WITH LOVE

Merry Christmas to you
One and all
All my brother and sister souls
Children who walk the earth together
As our lives and dreams unfold.

I'm told
That Christmas is a time to give
A time for family.
A time to joyfully, thankfully live
But it ain't always that easy...

And so
Although I know
We aren't by blood related
I want to send my love and care
And love – I really mean it.

We are the family of the world
Each one of us a shining pearl
And each with different things to give
And each with different ways to live.

And recently I've learned
That we all
Have an angel
Looking down and loving us
Not judging us
Just loving us
And always looking after us –
Who never will desert us.

Even when it's hard
To see and feel this love
I promise you this love exists
All around you and above.

And in the eyes of God
(Whoever He or She may be)
Each one of us is equal
Throughout humanity.

We are the glowing fruits of life
Our future shining in our eyes
We have our hearts
We have our minds
And we can leave the past behind
And make a difference to mankind
And peace and beauty we will find.

All we have to do is love
And trust and give, to really live
And thank for all the little things
(You know, I'm not talking
'Bout diamond rings).

Thank for our friends
Thank for this life
Thank for the trees
And the sun's yellow light
Thank for our hearts
Thank for our dreams
Thank for each day
No matter how hard it seems.

I wish to say I love you.
You are my human other.
We all deserve a place in life
And shelter to take cover.

So I wrap my arms
Around your soul
And kiss your head
And hold you close
And hold you tight
And send you light
And trust that you will be all right.

Merry Christmas my sweet child
All my brother and sister souls
Children who walk the earth together
As our lives and dreams unfold.

## A FLEETING VISIT TO NORTH WALES

A million strokes abrush the sky
As ancient pine trees stretch on high
Then through the blue an eagle flies –
Reminds of times long gone.

A thousand sheep dot white on green
Their cloud-like puffs pervade the scene
Vast mists roll by as eagles scream –
Remind of ghostly song.

The lifetimes lost and aeons found
Yet still I stride o'er holy ground
I hark the angels' deafening sound
As for the past I long.

ΑΠΟΡΡΙΜΜΑΤΑ
LITTER

## A LITTLE RESPECT

Why do you insist
On treating me like this?
If not as if I'm asking for
A bed of scented roses
Or glowing dedicated proses
And I certainly don't need
A kiss
Or pat on the head
From the patronage of your
Grand hand.

Just a little simple respect.
Wouldn't you expect
The same?
In fact
Just that –
Wouldn't you demand?

And by the way...

A little clear
Consistent
Considerate
Communication
Goes a very long way –
Wouldn't you say?

So shall we start to play fair
For a change
Within a new
Mutually respectful exchange?
Our relationship
Can be easily rearranged.

Lets see.
Do you agree?
It's up to you
My dear
To choose
To start anew
With me.

## A MUTUAL LESSON IN HUMAN INTERACTION

Thank you
For helping me
To help myself today
When I politely came beside you
And enquired if I could briefly
Just impede your quiet view
To take a photograph or two.
You answered me:
"Whatever"
And I thought:
"How very rude."

So below
Whilst taking images
Of endless broken bridges
I resolved I would be strong
I would be tough, I would be rigid
Not to try to be polite
When I would walk back by your side –
To make my point and keep my pride.

So I put my dark shades on
Raised my chin
And carried on
Pursed my lips
Held straight my hips
Sang a silent steadfast song…

And then
Just when
I'd nearly passed
And you were not quite out of view
You turned
And smiled
And nicely asked
If photo taking was my task!

I replied
(With inner smile)
That my task was this and writing
And I'd come to Aberystwyth
For a visit
And a bit of inspiring…

And we shyly smiled
Each to the other
You said
"Well, good for you"
And I thanked you as I carried on
And left you to
Your peaceful view.

Yes I came to Aberystwyth
For a visit
And a photo
But did not know
That the day would show
Another way
For me to go.

I think
We both
Had many things
Weighing deeply on our thoughts.
I learned
That smiles are not a given –
With smiles respect cannot be bought.

I think you learned
A bit as well
I think we'll both reflect on this…
I wasn't expecting quite such a lesson
In the intricacies
Of human interaction.

## A PENNY FROM PAUL

A penny from Paul
For John to keep
And nevertheless
John sweetly sleeps
And as Paul weeps
He counts the cost
But John still keeps
The coin Paul lost.

A decade passed
And John sits high
To climb the ladder
Paul still tries
And John laughs hard
As coins abound
He's played his cards –
He chose his hand.

A decade more
And we await
The hand of fate
To turn the score
And sure enough
As John still laughs
A new age enters
Through the door…

And suddenly
Paul starts to rise
And shine before
Our very eyes
And John begins
To slip back down –
His laugh becomes
A worried frown…

As Paul climbs on
Towards the sun
Our falling John
From shadows runs
And as he hides
From haunted deeds
He falls upon
His knocking knees.

Where now to turn?
To whom to go?
He's lost it all
His friends depart
And as he searches
Through his heart
His bloody conscience
Turns to Paul.

The moral to
This testing tale?
That you must live
By your own name –
Yet still can choose
The path to take
And can your dreams
Or nightmares make.

And whether you're
A John or Paul
And live your life
To take or give –
Money will not
Fix it all
And love's the key
To really live.

# A VALIANT LIFE

To survive
Through testing times
And make it through
To the other side
Is the mark
Of a valiant life.

My child, you made it through this life
And you still stand here tall today
You struggled long and times were tough
You know, sometimes that's just the way.

You've proved your worth
With every stride
Despite the hurt
You've held inside
You made it through
To the other side
And stand here proud
And tall and strong
Yes, to this earth you do belong.

And others would have crumbled
Underneath the weight you bore
And others would have tumbled down,
Forgotten how to care.

And other people would have let
The ugly taint their soul
And other people would have left
The rightful path on which to go.
And others would have let it cost
The shining of their light
And others would have given up
That painful, valiant fight.

Let go, let go
Let go, my dear
Of the pain
You've held on much too near
To your sweet heart –
You can depart
From those sad days...
Oh! Do not let them hold you down
But still stand strong
And wear your crown.

No matter the hurdles
That life will throw
Each one
We overcome
Enables us to grow
And gives the opportunity
For our character to show.

In this life
We play our parts
Few are easy
Most are hard –
It's the path
Fate dealt our way
And the game
We had to play.

And each struggle
Was a gift
That allowed
Our soul to lift
And each challenge
Was a test
To help us rise above the rest.

And you've proved
Your strength and might
And you've proved
Your right to life
And you've shown
How you have grown
And you'll reap those
Seeds you've sewn.

Congratulations!
You're still here.
And celebrations!
You still care.

For to survive
Through testing times
And make it through
To the other side
Is the mark
Of a valiant life –
You can be very proud, my child.

## ALL

If
All
I
Had
Was
Me
Would
I
Be
Enough?

## AMAZING THINGS

Life. It's a beautiful thing.
To be greeted every morning
By the singing of the birds
Who each dawning herald happiness
For humankind to hear
With their grace they raise the skies
To remind the quiet mind
That if we listen close
And look around
We'll find
Amazing things.

As they sing they rouse the insects
To a dance around the garden
And the ardent loving buzzing
Sends a buzz that life's amazing
As the dragonflies dart by
Flirting with the butterflies
They remind that if we try
To search for beauty
We will find
Amazing things.

# AND THEY ROARED

They made their steadfast way
Through the swarming red sea streets
All smiling
All brothers at ease
Even the women
Cracking jokes with one another
And even those on the other side.
But tense.
This one was a big one.
And the Autumn before didn't bode well
For success
If we're truthful. That's probably the score.

But we were never that cold about it.
Clinical - I think that's the term to use.
They wear their hearts on their sleeves
You see
The current Gods
And the worshipers of course.
So still they stride
Towards the sacred place
Ever confident forwards in red
Expecting the win
Even if they don't believe in it;
Believing in the win
Even if they don't expect it.

The Dragon's gold is always there for the taking
Resting in wait amidst the holy mountains
To be claimed by the victorious
And the dedicated.
Here,
That's everyone.
Today, this massive little land
Joins together in union as only they can
To become a band
Of brothers and sisters,
Fighting for the same eternal cause.
Those jerseys might as well be
Their blood
Ironed out across their heroes' chests.
The sweet deliverers upon whom
Their entire future rests.
And the nation expects
Delivery.

And then the whistle blows.

And every beaming factory man
And booming business man
And dragon-stamped tiny child
And atmosphere tipsy nan
Leans forwards.
And it has begun.

And at the end
The God
In slow motion red
Dives
Through suspended space and time
And lilts of hymns and arias
Hanging high on the expectant breeze
Beneath the sheep shaped clouds
And places it firmly down
On the gracious golden grass.

The stadium for a split second paused
To understand the implications
The magnitude of the moment
And realisation of their dreams.

Then they leaped euphorically as one
To their mighty dragon's feet.

The treasure and glory was theirs.

And they roared.

## ANGEL

Angel ~ soft ~ so soft you whisper
Gently ~ tender ~ firm as honey
Wondrous mystery of presence
Fill ~ my soul ~ to effervescence
Indescribable emotion ~ glow
This glow ~ so sweet ~ so warm
So soft – that word
As ~ soft ~ as feathers
Wings ~ these wings
The touch of ethers
Warm ~ the majesty of love surrounding
From above ~ within ~ without ~ confounding
Logic ~ that ~ no longer needed
Greater logos felt ~ and heeded
Now ~ the dawn of some new splendour
Breaks ~ as heralded by yonder
Singing choirs ~ of winged ones
And harpists ~ bold in love magnificent
Yet tender ~ Oh! ~ so soft ~ again that word
It whispers lovingly and so ~ so sweet
As only nightingales and larks are heard
As when the silent glorious fireworks burst
When star-struck lovers meet
And feathers fall to rest on emerald grass
With kisses ~ white-winged miracles
Of wondrous healing bliss ~ the lift
That lifting ~ soaring ~ of my soul
Expansion ~ deep within ~ and through
Way out ~ amidst the holy stars I mingle
Awestruck ~ with your magnitude ~ I tingle
Wrap your holy wings ~ around this body
For such tender love as yours ~ I'm ready
So blessed ~ I am ~ by your holy visit
Open true and strong ~ my yearning spirit
Open wide ~ my waiting soul
Show ~ the shining path to my redemption
As your love light glows ~ in pure white gold
And magnifies ~ magnificent ~ my divine comprehension
As I feel ~ your love light ~ warm envelop
Hear your notes ~ the symphony
The star shone miracle ~ of love
Unspoken ~ far beyond ~ my humble earthly understanding
Yet so calm ~ complete ~ and utter knowing
Feeling strong ~ as strong as castles
Fairy castles ~ in eternity of space
Illuminated ~ open ~ by your sun shone ~ holy grace
In enlightened contemplation ~ being
Breathing ~ seeing ~ feeling ~ one
The awesomeness ~ of life ~ new life begun
More wondrous than ~ most beautiful of songs
That e'er were sang ~ how overwhelming sweet
And soft ~ and clear ~ those angel bells they ring
And your voice ~ as strong as flowers
And your heart ~ rains rainbow showers
And your love ~ it warms ~ like Heaven's fires
Sets alight ~ my soul's desires
As I wake ~ and Heaven shimmers
As the dawn of golden morning ~ being born
In bright new consciousness ~ it glimmers
Glimmer you ~ throughout my star struck soul
I kneel ~ upon these limbs ~ as more ~ your love
It still unfolds ~ your arms ~ and wings ~ these wings
They hold me ~ in their all consuming
Mighty love ~ you hold me
In a star ray ~ ray of sunlight ~ moon light
Love light ~ soul light ~ love light from above
And as the glowing ~ knowing ~ dawning
Of miraculous ~ new morning ~ fresh
I wake ~ in grace ~ from your embrace
A smile ~ of wonder ~ on my face
As clean ~ as flowerbud ~ shining new
As free ~ as lark ~ I fly through blue
New world ~ all changed ~ all crystal clear
In knowledge ~ that you hold me near
Each blessed day ~ through constant time
As I am yours ~ so you are mine
Our lives ~ our energies entwined
Us side by side ~ eternally
Each moment ~ in infinity
In peace ~ in perfect harmony
Within ~ without ~ below ~ above
In body ~ soul ~ in mind ~ in heart
As one ~ in light
In love.

## ANOTHER HAT

Another hat
Another head
Another day
Another way
Another way for me
To face the race
To meet outside
The other faces
Free my mind
From past disgraces
Lick my lips
Untie my laces
Free to find
To peep
From behind
The rim
To sing
To shine within
My hat today
She radiates
The mystery
Of my hidden face
She glows
My soul
She shows
Below
I know
I feel
That I am real
My hat
She hides
My soul still shines
She paints
The way
And paves the day
And waves away
Old hues of blues...

Today
A new bright hat I choose.
Tomorrow I will buy the shoes.

## AS I WALK

As I walk
Through the sunshine
Of the valleys
Of life
I will not feel
Any fear.
For I am with me
So I know
That Heaven's always near.

As I bask
In the sunshine
Of the garden
Of life
I will not feel
Any pain.
The light shines down
And the green grows 'round
And my hurt is washed away by the rain.

As I stroll
Into sunshine
Along the beaches
Of life
I will not feel
Any sorrow.
The tracks in the sand
And love holding my hand
Lead me joyfully into tomorrow.

## AS WE GAZE

As we gaze out on the green
As our eyes behold the scene
As we strive to look beyond
As we count each minute gone
As we ponder at the path
Stretching out in front of us
As we smile, or dare to laugh
Feeling that we're on the cusp.
As we wish to start anew
As we take a deep breath in
As we dream we wish we knew
How the future would begin.
As we contemplate a step
As we check our watch again
As we check our secret's kept
As we exercise refrain
As we yearn to venture out
As we gasp to breathe the air
As we ache to sing and shout
And banish all our fears and cares...

As we wait
And hesitate
As we stand
This old ground
As we dig
Our heels in
Life waits for us to begin.

## AT OUR FEET

Each day of life
We struggle sweet
To read the message
At our feet.

AUTUMN

I want to be as free as Autumn plains
Where long cast shades convey a season gained
As Summer's rot makes magic from decay
And birds fly by on Northern lighted way.

I long to strong crop gather harvest fruits
And pave the way for fresh-sprigged young green shoots
Before the starving winter comes to loot
And cooling blue-tinged sun makes her retreat.

I yearn to yellow-lighted cut my path
Through fields of corn awaiting freeing swathe
To outrospect, reflect on giving graft
And thank for seeds I sewed for yields that last.

I smile to slide through slip'ry golden leaves
Which help the hedgehogs fat the worms retrieve
Who heap the birds with hope and breathe belief
That sun again will be in Spring unsheathed.

I sing to skip through crackling bonfire fields
Whilst on my skin the light delightful feels
As tingling as the sparkling sapling peels
Anticipating future forest yields.

I love to dance amidst the mists of gold
Imagine dancing in the days of old
Imagine hidden harvest tales untold
Before the mighty forest lands were sold.

## BEAUTY IS ONLY SKIN DEEP

Beauty is only skin deep
It's a bit like sheering a sheep.
You scrape off the fur
And behold! What lies there -
But exactly the same showing sheep.

Beauty is only skin deep
It's exactly like sheering a sheep.
You pull off the wool
And the soul you behold
Is exactly the same shining sheep.

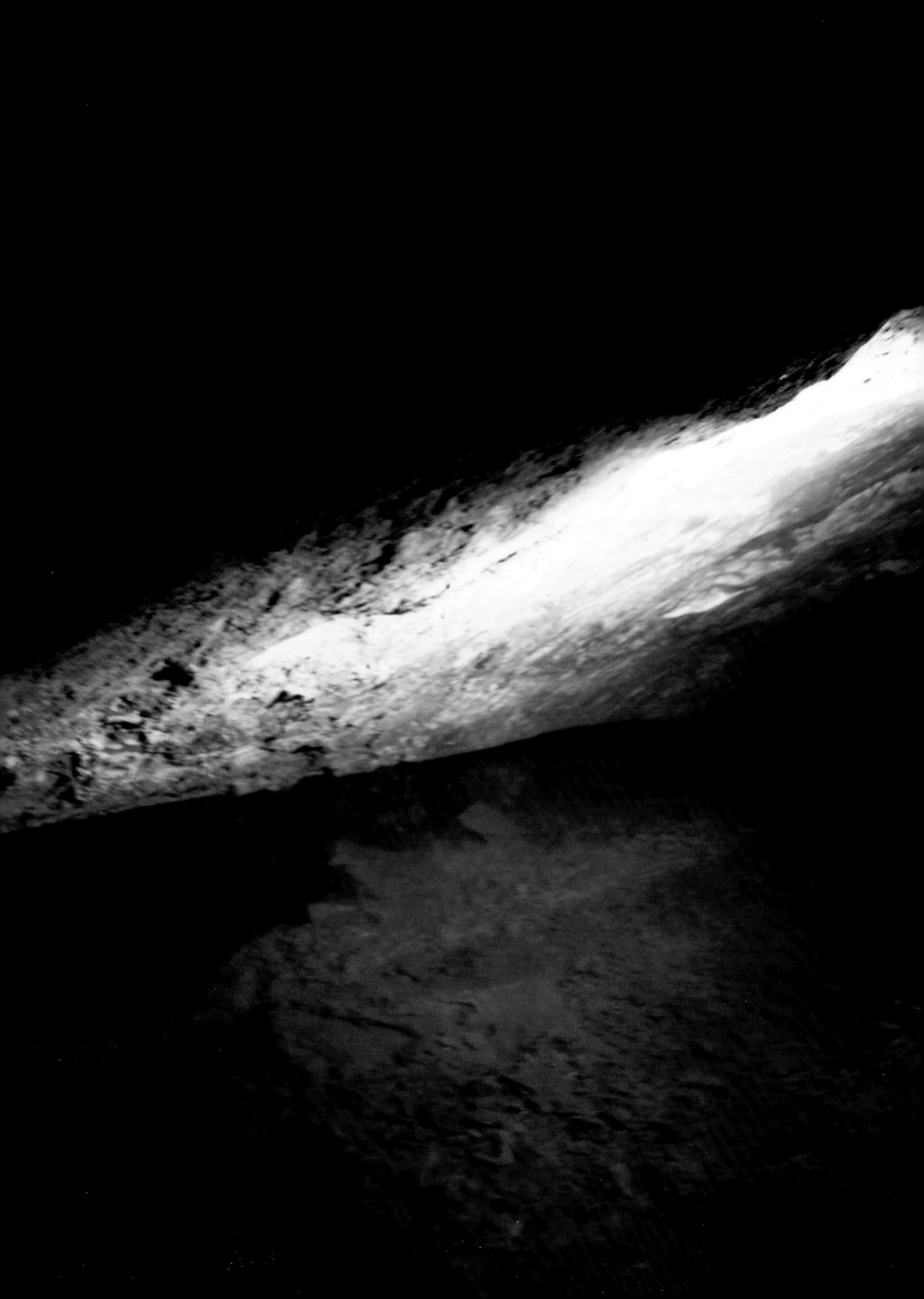

## BELIEF LOST

The emptiness of Nothing
Like a black, gaping void
Through which belief has fallen
Unavoidably destroyed
By crushing vortex vacuums
A spaceless time continuum
The placelessness of my oblivion
And gracelessness of past communion
And facelessness of past believing
Willingly suspended by my self deceiving
Then departed seeing, wrenched asunder
From the comfort zone of hope and wonder.

Now plundered dreams
And soundless screams
Replace the space
Of faithful face
And dark embrace
The futile race
To nightmares chase
Through my disgrace.

As minutes tick
And sorrow sticks
The hope I lost
Clocks up the cost
Of my belief
Transformed to grief.

Would that a tiny flicker of light
Impede upon my darkest night
And reignite the smallest might
To give me energy to fight.

## BELIEVE

Anything is possible
Attainable
Achievable.

There's just one rule –
The goal must be
Unto yourself
Believable.

BEND

For those of us who love the light
Internal extrospective plight
Form is of no mortal issue
Size and matter are but tissue.

For those of us who strain our necks
Growth beckons
Fate reckons
As we bend towards the sun
Nature feeds everyone.

BENEATH THE SNOW

Hush of snow
Ages old
Days unfold
Tales untold.

Passers by
Hear the cries
Secrets lie
Beneath the white.

## BLOWN

I am blown by the wind
And intricacies of my mind
Pursuing fated paths that wind
Interjected, intertwined
With brief encounters of humankind.
Delighting not in all I find
Yet always seeking light and joy
Inner strength and might
To fight
Enjoy the plight
Of following these roads
This road
My internal, eternal abode.
This winding path of joy and strife
Behind me the sweet wind
In front of me my life.

## BORN FREE

Born free
And imprisoned more
Each day we live.
Surely something's
Got to give?
A light flight back
To our aching wings;
A little song back
To us birds
Who yearn to sing;
A little might back
To raise our arms again;
A little fight back
To stride our way through pain;
A little sight back
That we can see past prison bars
And still keep searching for the stars
And not be ruled by fears and cares
And not be chased by dark nightmares.

In prison cells we needn't hide
The truth is buried in our minds
The gold is glowing in our souls
And future holds vast depths untold.

Turog
Bread
POBYDD BAKER
Christine Gough

## BREAD OF LIFE

Bread of Heaven
Bread of life
Soul of my village
My community born.
Warm, dry food of life
Of love, of peace
And hope in war.
Keep on baking
Keep baking togetherness
To feed Love's stomach –
Baking, creating, incubating
Hope, warmth, joy, love.

Let us share bread so sweet
We eat life's bread
When we meet
At your door
At your feet
On your path
In awe
At the joy of food we eat.
And let us not forget
Our days gone by –
Days of love
Comprised of wheat and rye.
Keep on baking
Keep baking life's food
And feeding Love's stomach –
Baking, creating, incubating
Hope, warmth, joy, love.

## CARIAD

We live in weird wild wispy willowed
Songbird swallowed
Wonderful Wales
Where dales so humble
Slumber under
Mighty mountains
Framed by vales
And aged mists
Rise from the green;
Where beasts roamed wild
Invaders tried
To wrench us from our land
(You know, they can't);
Where giants slew
And eagles flew
O'er forests stretching
Beyond the horizon;
Where rainbows hang
O'er blessed lands
And choirboys sang
In the language of heaven;
Where hiraeth spills
From golden hills
And black gold seams
Shine from those same hills;
Majestic cliffs
Retreat to meet
The blue sea lapping
At their feet
And mirrored lakes
For beauty's sake
Reflect the sun
Each dawn begun
Reflect exquisite
Dancing leaves
That quiver in
The season's breeze;
Oh! Why do you want, my child, to leave
When we live in a land so wild and sweet?

## CELEBRATING LILIES

Lillies ~ shining ~ celebrate! ~ break through ~ to new ~
to glowing colour ~ life ~ and raindrops ~ dancing over ~
sunlit orange ~ soothing pinks ~ and red ~ blood red ~
the hue ~ of passion ~ life ~ and fire ~ and revolution ~
melting into ~ golden yellow ~ strong ~ the colour of daffodils ~
that shine upon ~ the golden hills ~ and burst ~ each day anew ~
and fresh ~ as overhead ~ in peace ~ in love ~ in contemplation ~
revelation ~ celebration ~ emanation ~ joy it spills ~ from sunlit hills ~
and lovely lillies ~ singing splendour ~ born again ~ in love ~ so tender ~
glow more radiant ~ by the hour ~ thank you ~ for this gorgeous flower.

## CHANGE

Change…

It's the primary constant that exists.
And the second is that mankind will resist.

But to achieve a real state of evolution

Surely

Would be

That we

Embrace our fundamental right of revolution.

For it's only when we challenge set beliefs
That we stride on forwards and we can achieve.

CREAM LIQUEUR
of cream
finest Welsh

## CHERISH THE OLD

Cherish the Old
Great ancestors of our landscape.
Cherish the Old
Great travellers through our seascape.
Cherish the beauty
That radiates through their journeys.
Cherish the Old
Great founders of our dreamscape.

A jaded vase
Protective as an ancient Chinese rhyme;
Tall ticking clock
And well worn shoes - His footsteps plod in time.
A shining fruit bowl
Holding soul fruit
Sitting wise and wild;
And candlesticks -
The warm glow flicks
And shines Her light on nurtured child.

An antique frame
That sits on high
And holds vast memories from the sky;
A soul so deep
Their secrets keep
As generations watch on high;
Experience – the golden tool
From ones who understand life's rules
And innocence – from past times blessed
Imbued with wafts of frankincense.

Oh! Cherish the light
That manifests
Through gorgeous crinkled eyes.
Cherish delights
That come in form
Of rhubarb crumble pies.
Cherish the love
That holds you so dear
And always, wish granted, will hold you so near.
Cherish the life
That shines through those eyes
And remember, my Child,
Thanks to them -
You are here.

## CHILDREN OF THE WORLD

Children of the world unite.
Yours is the future
Of life's great fight.
Yours is the duty
To put things right.
Children of the world
Unite!

Please
take
your
litter
home

## CHOICES

If my future years hold the essence of my dreams
Now, I am living the path to their fulfilment.
Only my choices dictate
Whether my dreams I'll create.

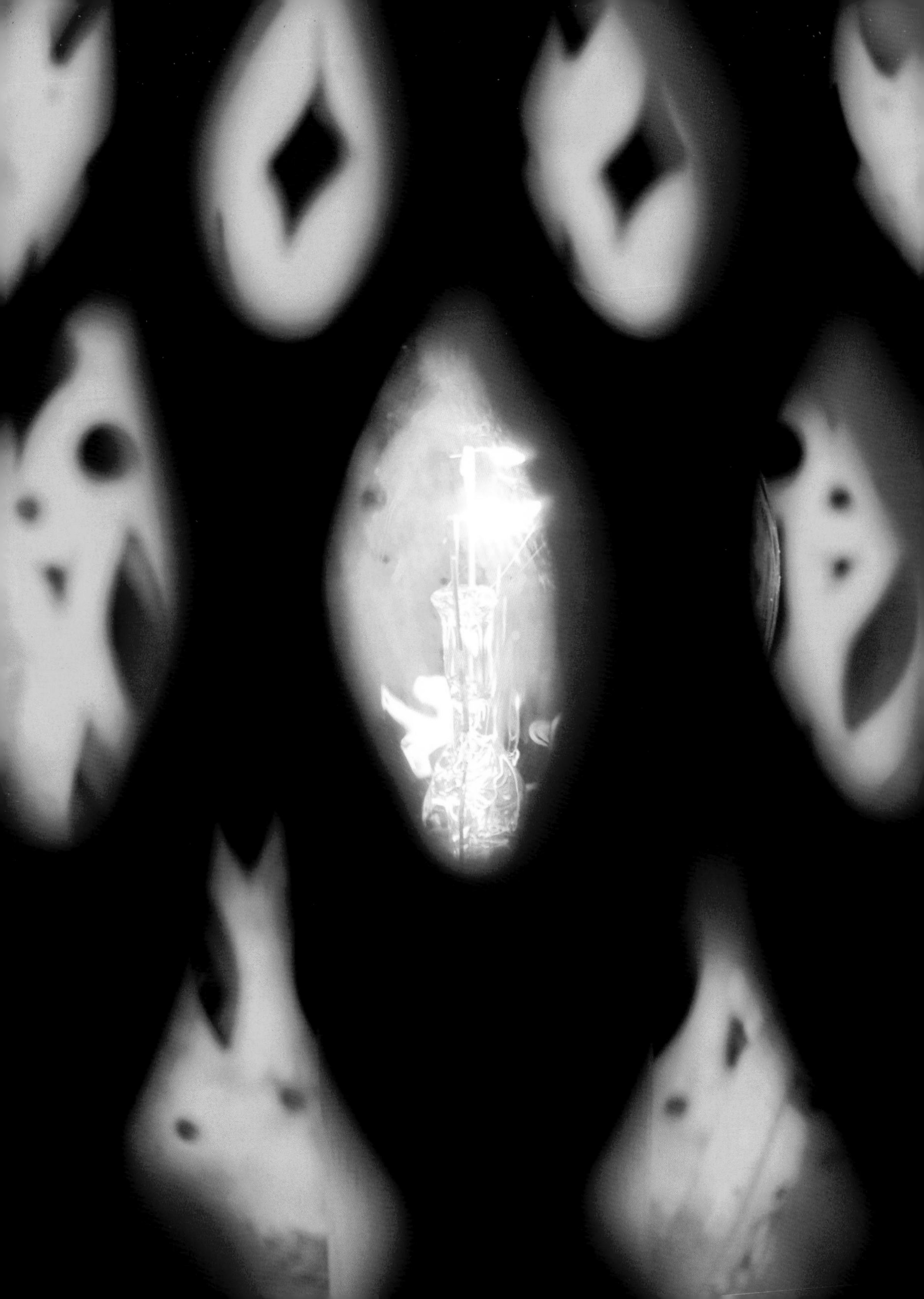

## CHOOSE ME

Let it be me
For I can see
Beyond the ancient mystery.

Choose me
For I can find
The truth that's buried in your mind.

Choose me
For I perceive
The weakness in the plans conceived.

Choose me
For I believe
And know the path to your reprieve.

Choose not
The other one
Whose false smile shines like setting sun.

Choose not
The friendly face
Whose wide eyes search for your disgrace.

Choose not
The foe held dear
Who speaks the words you want to hear.

Choose me
And do not fear
I'll hold your hand and keep you near.

## COME FLY WITH ME

Freedom for society
Come fly with me
Come fly, be free!
Question the hypocrisy
Democracy
Of make believe.
People die and fat cats lie
To challenge our beliefs in life
The planet sighs
And all the while
We pay for it in blood and strife.
Trees are dying
They're still lying
Lakes are drying
Desserts frying
Planet's gasping
Why? We're asking
Bees are dying
Still not trying
Ice is melting
Waves are belting
Shores and coastlines
But they don't mind –
Oil's still flowing
Gold's still glowing
Planes still going –
God save human kind.
Freedom for society
Come fly with me
Come fly, be free!
Question our society
The webs they weave
From make believe.
Freedom for community
It must be us
We still believe
We must achieve
Our last reprieve
We must break free
Come fly with me!

## CRUEL WORLD

It's a cruel world.
One which sets us up to fall
After raising us to reach for heights
Above, beyond, within our grasp –
Yet somehow not in sight.
They tell us try again, keep strong
If at first we don't succeed
Yet we'll succeed
If we believe
With God our Father's help along
Provided we first help ourselves –
Then to the flock we can belong.

So I wait to see
My still stone bleed
And fool myself that I still believe
And pray to God
To give me strength
To try again
And help myself
To still be strong
And carry on
Lest I get left upon life's shelf.

Cwtch Cottage

## CWTCH COTTAGE

Cwtch Cottage
I arrive at sweet Cwtch Cottage
And she opens up the door.
She sees my face
It betrays my disgrace
She smiles.
And beckons me inside.
The scent of fresh ground coffee roasting
Curls through sweet patchouli air
And basil pot upon the shelf
Bestows another dimension.
Age-old comprehension
Waits
As I settle in the chair.
And fiddle with my hair.
Confession spills
Like wine
It sploshes into the open glass;
And still she smiles
Even while I cry
And just one question asks:
"And how do *you feel* about that?"

I leave some hours later
With a smile –
A smile so wide!
I couldn't even tell you of
The miracles
That did go on
For those sweet hours inside.

## CYCLES

I raise my head to sky and thank with praise
For miracles the universe bestows;
As cyclical as are the age-old ways,
White Winter's path of death makes way for growth.

## DANCE

My Grandmother once told me:

My Child
You were born to dance.

Why else would you have feet
*and* be able to hear music?

Well
I couldn't argue with her.

## DEWDROP

Each dream-fed day I rise anew
As fresh and poised as morning dew
To glimmer in the golden dawn
And quiver filled with hope reborn.
As mystic mauves melt into reds
And orange skyline morphs to blue
I gaze at distant flowers' heads
And whisper "To thyself be true".
A little bubble on a blaze
Amidst a universe of grass
Horizon-filling everglade
On land a billion times more vast.

And gracefully time passes on
While we cling to the rooted ground
As constant as each breaking dawn
As vast as lifetimes lost and found
As fierce as the winter morn
Inexorably time moves on
While we remain upon our lawn
And gaze at fields and worlds beyond.

## DON'T BE A SHEEP

Don't be a sheep
Lost in snow
Wondering where to go
With no leader
Or hands to feed ya.

Don't plod around
Waiting for the call
Without a sound
Within walls
And no idea at all.

Don't be a sheep.
The world is full enough
Of sheep
The meek
Who only nod and bleat.

Step up.
Speak up.
Don't be weak.
No offense to sheep.

DROP YOUR MASK

Drop your mask
Sometimes
Just a bit
Once in a while
For those few
You know or meet
Who deserve
A peek at your face –
Those true few who
Will love your face
Better than the mask
Which hides the real you –
The persona in your place.
The world misses you
When you're not around
She really loves you
And needs you to be who you are.
Although the mask is fine
It lacks your beauty
It's no comparison or reflection;
Commonplace
It's just a folly
Where once a castle stood
And now denies your right
To be loved and understood
As you are
Without the care
Of being judged.
Take it off
Sometimes
Gradually at first
And only for a few –
The deserving who will not judge you
But only love you
For being you.
Then the more you drop your mask
And show your real face
The more others will drop theirs
And more real faces you will meet.

## DUSKY CARDIFF STREETS

Steely misted shadowed streets
Half lit by lamps
Ungraced by feet
At this, the dusky hour of eve
When day has died
And night unrisen
Early dewdrops rest and glisten
Not a sound unless you listen
Granted by the ghosts' permission.
Silver grey the mists obeyed
And ethers closed out creamy day
When shoppers strolled their lunch away
Their trip to town to spend the day
Then, maximising amber light
The carefree streetwise children played
Before Mam called them in for night
Hiding pointless, try as might
And long before the living night
When rowdy revellers appear
Inebriated, drunk delight
For all who want
And not – to hear
And foxes slink through alleyways
Watched only by the bats and owls
And tortured souls
Join dancing girls
To let loose deep primeval howls.
Now all are in, to rest in homes
Relaxing on their telly thrones
Once light has left
And sun has fled
And tiny babes engulfed in bed
The family all wrapped and warm
Until tomorrow's bracing dawn
They sit at home and talk and eat
Dissolve the day as they unwind
And eve descends on Citykind –
The alter-ego of the day;
Still, I alone on silent feet
Walk on through dusky Cardiff streets.

## ENJOY

If my future years hold the essence of my dreams
Now, I am living the path to their fulfilment.
So – to enjoy the path!
To Live! Love! Laugh!

## EVERY DAY

Every day that I pass through
I'm thinking about you.

Every time I see your smile
I thank my stars for you.

Every place without your face
I wonder how you are.

Every hour I shower love
It's cos I really care.

I don't have money, don't have power
All I have is love and flowers

So I send my heart upon my sleeve
And soft white feathers from above

Because, my friend, I do believe
That you and I are bound by Love.

## FAITH

I have faith that the sun will rise each day
I have faith that the young will laugh and play
I have faith that love always will show me the way
I have faith in my loved ones and I.

I have faith that there's more to this lifetime of ours
I have faith that believing will soon open doors
I have faith that this cosmos is my home and yours
I have faith that there's magic and beauty in store.

I have faith in the testing decisions I'll make
I have faith I can separate real from fake
I have faith there'll be changes and changes I'll make
I have faith I'll have chances and chances I'll take.

I have faith in the past and will have no regrets
I have faith in my dreams, they will be achieved yet
I have faith in each dawn and the truth it begets
I have faith that my actions can still make amends.

I have faith there's a reason that I am here now
I have faith there are many things that I must do
I have faith my experience and wisdom will show
I have faith there are many great things that I know.

I have faith in my courage and faith in my strength
I have faith that sweet love will prevail in the end
I have faith in my family and faith in my friends
I have faith that the beauty of life never ends.

I have faith I will shine through the darkest of nights
I have faith in the power and beauty of light
I have faith that sweet freedom is my divine right
I have faith that my soul will be risen to flight.

## FAMILY

The love
Of a good Mother
A Father
Sister
Brother
Is love that's like no other –
A roof that gives us cover;
A home that gives us shelter
When life is helter-skelter
And arms that wrap around us
When those outside confound us.

## FAT CAT ATTACK

So glad I live in a democracy
Land of the free.
I believe.
Streets all paved with equality
Paupers and Princes hang with me
No such thing as poverty
It's all in the mind you see...

The rich get richer
The poor get worse
Struggling on
Debt immersed
Vicious circle like a curse
And fat cats laugh with bulging purse
No inclination to reverse
Their profit
From the poor man's hearse.

Corporations
Got our nations
In a strangle hold
Yet we spend for our lives
Sell our values of old
Then they move somewhere cheaper
And we're all on the dole
Reminding ourselves
All that glitters ain't gold
And the chair gets twenty million
For a bonus we're told.

We make it, buy it
Die from it
It's their ammunition.
Their quest for profit puts us
In a dangerous position
Fat wallets lined
On the back of human extinction
And blood for oil –
The whole world weeps
For fat cats' decisions.

It's a fat cat attack
And you'd better panic
Might be four or five
Hiding up in your attic
Crouching behind
The company plastic
White men in grey suits
And they're bloody ecstatic
They're counting our money
And it just isn't funny
It's a fat cat attack
Better panic
It's drastic.

## FEAR

Fear
Binds a ring of anger through our hearts
Departs us from our true and reasoned sight
Third sight of knowing all will be alright
As false cruel voice just dread to us imparts.

Fear
Tortures babes and children's minds
And nurtures them in endless circled pain
When comfort from their parents they can't find
As shaking scared, the folks from love refrain.

Fear
Makes us hate our fellow souls
It even makes us hate the ones we love
As we deny our basic rights of old
And cower from rays of sun shone from above.

Fear
Like a cloak of endless night
Impedes upon the shining of our light
And like a clock of grief it grinds us down
By ticks and tricks we think we are alone.

Fear
Contrives to knock us down from flight
So soaring to the sun seems out of sight
And it denies our fundamental right
To shine through life with all our soul's sweet might.

I refuse to embrace
The fakery
Of fear.

I'm shaking that cloak off now.

## FLY

Let your wings spread and touch the sky
Words will be said and the old day will die
Keep on reaching
Stretch and strive
You were granted wings to fly.

Reach for the moon
Follow the sun
Smile as you walk
Laugh as you run!
Love as much as you possibly can
Flow with the wind, with the world in your hands.

Follow your dreams
Seek out the light
Release the delight
Of your might held inside
Of your passion unbridled, compassion rekindled
And fire ignited where hoping had dwindled.

Let your wings spread and touch the sky
The stage will be set and most will comply
So free your mind
And soar up high
Your soul and being yearn to fly
Take to sweet flight and you'll soon see why
Oh! Let your wings spread and touch the sky!

## FORGET IT

Worry worry
In a hurry
Pain on faces
Going places
People frowning
Children scowling
Grey surroundings
Concrete pounding
Walking faster
Working harder
Stress and strain
Surmounts the shoulders
Footsteps plodding
Sheep still nodding
Folks forgotten
Why they're here.

Concrete city
Iron trickery
Shaky promise
Wonky premise
Nothing sits right
Nothing feels right
Got to sit tight
Through this black night.

Worry worry
All a flurry
Fear reeks
Through hearts of many
Fear rules –
That dreaded tool,
It rules and fools –
We're schooled in terror.
What an error –
Why we let it,
Come on folks,
This fear –
Forget it.

## FORGET WE NOT

Forget we not
The aim is always growth
In mind, the shell and in our living souls.

Forget we not
To reach towards the light
And feed off crystal water streams below
By constant flow of day and darkest night.

And as things go
We can't forget
The point is always love
Which can be found within, around
And raining from above.

Forget we not
To laugh's the food of life
To cry's our right divine
This world is yours and mine
And as we picture it and shine
We'll be with loving arms always entwined.

Forget we not
That we are one
Forget we not
The game's begun
To make us think that we are twain
And cannot merge our hearts again;
Yet all we have to do as one
Is share our soil
Bestow our love
Stretch towards the warming sun
And thank the universe above.

## FRIEND

You shine so strong, so pure and true
As such a blessing in my life.
Your warm sweet loving, tender care
I lovingly accept forevermore
And give my love in turn to you –
This love of mine - 'tis ever yours.
What heavens opened,
Landed you beside me
All those years and dreams ago?
And yet, I opened up my eyes
And saw you standing there
With my soul
Both, our first foot on the stair –
To Love! This love!
It burns so bright
Like a million candles
Glowing through the velvet night.
This love, it overcomes all distance,
Time and space and all resistance.
Love, this love we share so strong
This love – 'tis our eternal song
And through the lyrics
Notes and rhythms
Undulating harmony
We sing together, waking songbirds
Flying, floating,
You and me.
Us, my friend
This flame will burn eternal
Fading never
Though for days we may not speak
It burns like stars
Goes on forever
Until us two again in person meet.
And friend - I will not say I miss you
Though a trickle seeps now down my cheek
For sure I know
As sure as every flower that e'er did grow
That you and I
Just like the stars
In this great sky
We shine divine
Us side by side
In eternity.
Yes, that's the way, my darling friend
Our love will always be.

TY MAWR
OR NIC
& "Fresh from
Great House
enny
Tel: 01873 840 7
APPLES
per bag
£1.20
COURGETTE
BEETROOT
CHARD

# FRUIT SELLER

Fruit Seller, Fruit Seller
Sell your wares to me!
And not just fruit –
But veggies too –
Anything that's green!
And if it's grown from local lands
Then honey, all the better
That cabbage and that butternut squash
Will go down well with a bit of Welsh butter.
And garlic bulbs! And pesto too!
Made from home grown rocket!
And basil, sage and parsley scents
From a garden that's glowing
Just over the fence…
And tomatoes!
I smell them!
Like tomatoes from childhood
Tomatoes from dreams –
You remember that smell?
And the raspberries, gooseberries
Strawberries, blueberries
Blackberry picking…
I remember it well!

Fruit Seller, Fruit Seller!
Sell me your wares!
My lips now all juicy
At the thought of that flavour!
Fruit seller, maybe an apple or two
Or banana for this humble poet to savour?
I know that it's tough,
We're all making a living
So Fruit Seller, do,
Be at your most forgiving…
I don't have a penny –
Of that I'll confess
But for an apple
I'll sing you
A song for the best!

FULL CIRCLE

It feels we have come full circle
Again
Even though the circle
Looks to me fragmented
Broken
Round
With gaps and missing pieces
Particles flying
Around the fraying edges
Still I wait
At its core.
And somehow it feels complete.
A journey – yes
'Tis life;
This circular perpendicular
Interchangeable
Exchange
We have, we live
We breathe
Between
Our strangers' walls.
This funny friendship game
An oftentimes unfunny strain
On my heart.
Oh! The senses!
It is the usual sensual senselessness
Within all the sense that I can make of it.
Life. It is what it is.
Our friendship leans
On the ethers
Of this fraying, flailing
Never-ending shape.
And somehow it feels complete.
How so?
Yet so it is.
It must just this, be us.
So still I stay at the core
Of this unconditional circle
Happy to be here
Happy you are there
Until the day
That you, my friend
Acknowledge your friend and hear.

## GIVE A LITTLE SUGAR

Feed me a little sugar
Come,
Give a little sugar
Please
As you sit here
And rest in ease
Gazing out at paradise
Pondering men and mice
Don't tease
Lift a little finger
Just give a little sugar
And help me please
To fly and live
You can release
My need, the purpose
To just survive and eat
And then I too
Like you
Can live
Fed, satisfied, fulfilled, complete.

## GO WITH THE FLOW

Go with the flow
Just don't fight the current
The reasons will show -
Will become apparent.
For as you've stayed here
Year through year
As you've lived here
Hour by hour...
You were born to tread this path
Yes! You were born to be a star.
When this, my friend, you do believe
Your sweetest dreams will be achieved.

GOLDEN BUBBLES

Walking onwards
We walk on
Each day we wake, it twists anew
We strike at dawn of each new moment
Each new lifetime, searching straight
As strong the great almighty trees
Grow steady still their canopies
And down below we search for seeds
We scattered long, so long ago
Before the breeze that picked them up and flew
Cross timelands, sandscapes
Mountain scree sides rivers streaming through
And bellows deep the orange molten gold that sweeps
Its path unseen, unheard, untold, unrevealed, concealed below.
The gold still flows in vast and gleaming steaming
Glacier gardens bubbling invisible through
The green green surface grass
On which, beneath the yellow sun we bask...
I ask when this illusion breaks and golden bubbles sweep up to the sky
That they remind us striding ants who step in time in line
The reasons why
This golden molten steaming shower
Holds the power of you and I.
Of us, of we, of all, of one
This earth and us upon her surface
Dance as golden truth set free
And life - new life – begun.

## GOLDFISH BOWL

To see the world
In a goldfish bowl –
To feel the waves
Drown dead her soul.

Us human fish
Glide round and round
Though killer things
And sharks abound
Too mind numbed dumb
To be appalled
Encased in endless
Concrete walls.

## GRAPEFRUIT

Life is short
Bitter sweet fruit to taste
But love will endure
And hope always prevails.
I don't want, sugar
Time to pass me by –
Short or days too long,
Bittersweet, let me eat
The fruits
The sustenance of life.
I don't want, honey
Through clouds not to fly –
Pure white or dark and low,
Over clouds I'll fly.
I'm alive
And I will soar through sky.

Sweet, so sweet, bitter fruit is life
Yes, I'll always want to eat
Grow, fly, live complete.
Soar through clouds and sky
Sweet freedom of life
Joy, strife, pain, delight
Such magnitude in being alive!
Don't want my time to pass me by
Though bitter sweet, the joy of life
I'm alive – won't let time pass me by
I'm alive, I soar
I'll soar through sky
Sweet bitter sweet
The fruits of life
Yes! I will eat each fruit I find!
I will soar!
I will fly!
Bitter sweet, I am alive!
I will live before I die
I will feast
On the fruits of life!

## HEAVEN IS IN HERE

I've searched so long
Searched far and wide
To find the light
I've held inside
My heart
My mind
My glowing soul
As on this path
I've travelled forth
Ever singing my sweet song
Trusting the light that guides me along.
I thank my stars I've understood
The message that lay at my feet
The rainbow that arched o'er my way
The meaning of each newborn day
And as I pray
And sunlight splays
Through cracks in leaves to light my way
I smile and close my eyes and say
Thank you
For
Heaven Is In Here.

## HER SPIRIT SPEAKS

Her spirit speaks
While chaos outside weeps
Still she stands strong
Still sings her song
The colours flow
While down below
All anguish rains
The river runs with tears and fears
Still sun
Shines on her hair
And through her soul
Her thoughts run deep
As smiling still she secrets keeps
She grows inside
Her heart expands
Beats strong and long and soft and wide
And those outside
They wonder how
They wonder why
And what she knows
As still they cower and cry
Yet still she smiles and glows.

## HOME

Home is where
The hearth is
And all concerned
Within its walls
Adorn the glow
Of embers slow
Warm and strong
We all belong
Within the light
Its tender might
A silent song
As darkness falls
And members called
Within its walls
The hearth, the heart
The burn, the yearn
To be within
To warm with kin
As outside carries on
Within her heart
We belong
Our heart, our hearth
Our home
Our song.

## HOPES AND DREAMS

Hopes and dreams
Hopes and dreams
They keep me floating
Soaring high
They squeeze each second
Melt each minute
Bursting through the rainbowed sky
As soft propelled towards the shining
Blinding sun
On angels' wings
I sing, I stretch, I reach I fly.
These tantalising, life inspiring
Hopes and dreams of mine
They are a shrine
One living, breathing, feeling
To the days I was a child
And life held only mystery
And future only bright and green
And to this day
It still would seem
That child lives on in me.
And why should we –
Should they suggest
That as we grow
Our dreams be laid to rest?
Not me!
Eternal as the constant ebb and flow
Of the great deep almighty sea
So shall my hoping never go
And shall these dreams live on in me
Live strong
Live long
Still be my song.
Why not?
For as I hope and dream
That child in me is free.

## HUMANITY

Humanity, humanity
I live, I breathe, I ache for thee
I love, have faith
I fly for thee
Humanity Humanity.

Humanity, humanity
I long for the day
That we will see
We're each
Just a tiny part of thee
Here
To live
In equality.

Humanity, humanity
We're each
Just a leaf
On this great tree
We sway together
Feed and breathe
Share drops of water
Soil and love
Together
We thrive
In the sunlight above
From below
Feed our soul
Rich our roots
Steeped in love.

Humanity, humanity
When will we wake
And start to see
That you are just
The same as me
That you and me
Are simply we
And one
We are
Beneath the sun
We glow and grow
And shine as one
The I
We find
In this great sky
Purely exists
In one true mind
One heart
One soul
One common goal.
Humanity –
It's Love alone.

## I AM A SOUL

I am a soul
With strength and might
Who's here to fight
That great good fight –
To find the light
Outside and in
Then follow it
As my life begins.

## I DON'T KNOW WHY I LOVE YOU BUT I DO

I don't know why I love you
But I do.

You
Light up fires within my soul
I never knew existed.
Offer help to warm my cold
Before I can enlist it.
Shower me with raining love
Most welcome hail from lands above
And clasp your hands around my heart
Eternally protect it.

You
Shine so brightly that I long to see
Show me how to find the light in me
Lead me to the truth and to reprieve
Offer me a lifetime where I'm free.

Give so much
And never count
Tender touch
And never shout.

Haunt my dreams
With angels' glow
So I awake
And truly know
You're there
And that you really care
And that together
We will grow.

I don't know why I love you but I must.
It's just
This song sounds like my love is just for me.
Its sounds as if I love just what you do
And that I love just your sweet love for me.

And yet
I do suspect and say
I love you all the more because you're you;
Because we've found our way in life together
Because I know this love will be forever.

Because
You show
Your wondrous side
In everything you do.
Because
You prove each hour I wake
My luck in having you.

I love your laugh
I love your smiles
I love the twinkle in your eyes
I love the love you give to me
I love this love that sets us free.

I do know why I love you
And I will
Forever and a day and lifetimes more
Yes, I will love your darling soul until
This soul of mine
Can love and feel no more.

# I FEEL SO LOST

I feel so lost
In time
This time
And the earth proceeds around me.
She entwines
Attempts to ground me
As I try
To float on high
But am never free.
Tied to the end of society's rope
Strong, yet deeply frayed
And limiting my scope
Grabbing me back
She circles my ankles
And tries to drown me.
My need to break free
But stay grounded
Confounds me.
Unrest, my soul
Why can't life allow me?
She is a cunning prison guard
I sit in a circle of glass shards
Transparent, but still they stop me
They reflect the sun
And dazzle
As the light burns
I frazzle
Smoke rises from my skin
I burn, I yearn from within
I am getting thin
And weary
I try and try to begin
But don't see
How I can.
I'm only human
But what does this mean?
When sustenance on earth
Grows lean
And nourishment from heaven
Grows sparing
Do I go on caring?
My body aches from trying
My wide eyes dried from crying
Though I know
This hell on earth
I'm sharing
With sisters and brothers
My frightened human others
Lost, confused friends and lovers
Birds who need to sing
With clipped, caged wings
Neutered cats and dogs
Proud trees chipped to logs.
God let us continue
This race that we started.
Give me the grace
To be wholehearted.
Part me from my anger
Let me keep on being stronger.
I'm still so alone
Please, throw this dog a bone
Give this cat another life
End the struggle of this strife
Cut me loose from within
My steely ring of glass
Cut this rope
Give me hope.
This is all I ask.

## I HAVE A QUESTION

I have a question
More massive than the sky.
Who am I?

As the turbined clouds slip
Roar their way away
To part the blue
A shooting round tumultuousity
Of being, flying, seeing
Passing overhead and promising to rain
Or shine the day
To let alive the sunshine silver ripples
Dancing through, across the fire-lit lakes
My heart aches with the choice
My voice
It quivers soft renditioning of broken constant
Whispering lullaby of sorts and always in the background
In the future notes I hear it
Feel it, gather up my soul and heart
To let them start
To now believe it.

## I WISH I WAS A DUCK

Life sucks.
I wish I was a duck.
Cos all they have to do
Is eat, sleep, swim
And fly and… quack.

Well, let's just say
That ducks
Have all the luck.

I WRITE FOR PEACE

I write for peace
That peace may shine a blessing on this land
On this sweet soil
This Mother Earth
We call our own.
I write that we may treat her so
With all the loving tender care
We'd show
To our own child
Or to our Mother dear.

I write for peace
That we may from our anger turn
That next the dawn
Will find us children
Celebrating every leaf
And every other
Mother's child.

I write for love
That we may to our other turn
To every brother, sister, other
Elder, younger
Our amazing others
And as we peer
Into the mirror
That the miracle of recognition
Like new dawn
Begins to glimmer
Creates a shiver
So soft and warm
And wonderful
And in truth she will appear
And by her grace
In our sweet other's face
And eyes
We find
Our own
One soul
And meeting of
One heart
One mind.

## IF MUSIC BE THE FOOD OF LOVE

If music be the food of love
Feed me 'til I want no more.
If music be the food of love
Open up the door
And let the melody ring true and loud
As sunshine breaking through the clouds
Let her notes engulf my being
Open wide my eyes to seeing
Open soft my throat to breathing
Open strong my heart to feeling.
Feel the rhythm beating through me
Feel the sweet pulsating move me
Hear the notes inspire to groove me
Feel the floating tune shake through me.
Beat, the drum and shiver, symbols
Violins play as the lark song
Trumpets cheer, fine flute fly clear
Ripple, golden magic harp song.
Hear those words!
They stir my spirit!
Move my feet to dancing joy
Click, my heels and tap, my fingers
Let me dance with every girl and boy.
Fill! My soul!
Laugh! My eyes!
Lift! My heart!
And raise the skies!
Let my body
Feel the music to its very core.
If music be the food of love
Feed me 'til I want no more.

## IMAGE IS IMPORTANT

Image is important
Perception so powerful
Understanding essential
But we
Will always
Be us.

## INDIVIDUALITY

Individuality:
The mark of me
For all to see.
I can't agree
That we should be
Just the same,
You and me.
My fingerprint –
There's only one
The same goes for
My toes and bum;
It's the choice
Of the free
And I'm happy
Being as me
As I can be.

## INSPIRATIONAL

Inspirational
Inspiration
Drives my soul
With the beating
Of her wings.
Inspiration sings.

So said the voice
Of the butterfly to the muse
Who blew the message on
Through the loving, subtle breeze
Who in turn shook her spirit
Through the glowing, shining leaves
Then as one landed softly
As a kiss between my ears.

# IT'S GOOD TO TALK

It's good to talk...
Let your feelings flow
Like ships a'sailing into calm
Calm waters blue and lightly shining
Glow
Just let it out and
Let it be
To shine just like the shining sea
Whose tranquil peace of mind
Still shimmers waiting
Right in front of you and me.
It's good to talk
Express the very best and worst
Of what we feel and how we feel it
What we see and how we see it
As we say the words
Still feeling through
To check that we
Still do believe it.

## JOIN

Poppy trees and Autumn leaves
Nodding, rustling in the breeze
Buzz-buzz buzzing bee believes
Hovering through flowers and leaves.

She walks through the parting grass
Sunlight falling on her skin
Light reflects and dances back
Emanating light within.

Strolling as the shadows cast
A glow upon her lovely hair
Then as she sighs, a butterfly
Appears through ethereal air.

She smiles and stops and looks ahead
While peals a gleaming strip of light
Illuminating petal beds
The sunset hot with gold ignites.

When further on along the path
Appears a figure standing tall
A silhouette with warrior's arms
As rays upon his wild hair fall.

He walks towards the maiden fair
Now smiling strong with knowing gaze
And as she waits, in light and grace
His strides embrace his future days.

In silent understanding song
The two join hands and turn as one
To carry on along their path
Towards the glowing, growing sun.

## JOYFUL

Joyful life you fill my soul
You soar through sunshine clouds aparting true
For you to clear the way that I may say
That I was born of light and live in love
Am always guided by the sweetest force above
And now, unlocked my heart, sweet shadows may depart
Their futile venture here and now
'Tis not for me - this one - to be o'ershadowed
No – no more fooled or cowed
By those tricks of your slick sticky, now unstuck illusion
I will suffer no - no more confusion
Now this pure true realisation provides the new solution
And this sweet beating heart sets free the mind that tried
To pull her down too long through its illusory guide
That was not set in truth - did not reside in love.
Today - the message from above is clear:
This life - so joyful, such sweet notes of music
For the heart to hear, such ripe delights of muses
For the eyes to see, such strong long tender soft belonging
Touches for the arms to bear - these gifts – the sweet perfumes
Of petal scented fragrances that lift our souls and senses far
Beyond the sky and lead us round and through
The starswept clouds and back again
To greet us with the reasons why
The very simple reasons why
We are alive -
For the sheer joy and love of life.

## KEEP MY LOVE

Filter out
Your stressful side
The restless mind
Of strife, of life;
Worry not
The hour is due
Your time is now
Your time of life;
The path is here
We cannot choose
The way to go,
The path will show;
Courage must
And needs abound
Internals found
The truth will out;

Struggle not
For life is short
And fun aborts
When needs alert;
Live the most
When pain hits worst
Drink life's joy
To quench your thirst;
Beware my child
For love is blind
And all paths wind,
The journey's hard;
Just keep your faith
And keep your hope
And keep my love
Locked in your heart.

## KEEPING GOING

Keeping going
Moving forwards
Walking on and on.
In a daydream
Sometimes nightmare
Singing song to song.
Keeping going
Through the heartache
Keeping showing
At each daybreak
Moving on
And edging closer
Inching forwards
Tighter, looser.
Moving onwards
Step by step
Paving over
Crack by crack
Ever smiling
Always trying
Still believing
Don't look back.

## LEADERS OF TOMORROW
## PICKING DAISIES IN THE SUN

In our little world of Wales
Pretty patch on quilted globe
We are blessed with mighty mountains
And with rolling, luscious glades
Where our young children play
Picking daisies to make crowns
Then the best golden daffs
To take straight back home to Mam
At the end of their day
Out drinking in the sun
Ernest playing and debating
Adventuring and contemplating
Laughing
Sharing life.
Just as we always taught them to.

The leaders of tomorrow,
Those innocent little ones.

God help them.
We must with love prepare them
For when the real journey comes.

Our little leaders of tomorrow
Picking daisies in the sun.

## LILAC FAIRY

Lilac fairy
Shining bright
Won't you light
My dreams tonight
Bless my sleep
As I sleep tight
Lilac fairy
Shining bright.

Shine your light
Through my sweet soul
Bless my future hours
And old
Kiss me as
My hand you hold
Keep me safe
From harm and cold.

Shine your light
Exude your glow
Cast your love
On me below
Grant me that
I'll always know
You're here with me
To keep me safe
Until upon the dawn I wake.

LLANSTEFFAN MUSES

The rolling winds obeyed the waiting sands
And calmed across the estuary
The waiting sea, her sweet commands
They rippled as a shiver through me
Walking free, I strode with sunshine at my back
Did not look back, just strode through shells
Dispelling long-past fears I'd held
Until those faded pictures
Melted as the birdsong into breeze
And rippling silver once again
Strong shone in front of me
And trees conspired to loves their leaves
Again and whisper to their freedom-seeking friends:
"Just don't look back, my love
You're watched upon, you see
By all the light and love you can imagine
From above, far more than just
The humble portion that these
Gleaming leaves reflect.
This notion I rest at your feet:
Your dreams you'll meet,
You'll live, one day
So just embrace
With joy, this path
Because, my child,
You're on your way."

## LOOK DOWN

Look down
To see the dazzling rays of sun
For they are shining in a modest pool.

Look round
To find your life has just begun
And by the superficial don't be fooled.

Look in
To see the truth that's lying deep
And realise you have the skills and tools.

Look up
To share the secrets you must keep
And let yourself be guided and be schooled.

Look true
To read the message at your feet
Remind yourself some signs you just must heed...

But know
That many obstacles you'll meet
And the answer's
Not always
The obvious.

## LOST IN MAY IN MY GARDEN

Dragonflies dart by with rapturous, dazzling flair
Fluorescent, translucent, glowing, sparkling,
Tri-colour dancing their ethereal unearthly joy.
The celebration of life, bursting, bursting life
Pushing through the ground, erupting from branches
Nature taking chances on fair weather
Sunny disposition daze, the haze
Of newborn days, a second chance at life
To start anew, as pure
Sparkling dew that glistens nestled
On a leaf, belief in hope,
A lifetime new
A time to show, to embrace and
Engage in Love
Dream making, earth shaking
Life creating
Celebrating
New creation.

As new
And
As old
Constant
Magical as dreams
As tales of aged oaks and unicorns
Centuries of allure that we recall
To faintest memory - a glimpse back for and from the soul
To a window far forgotten, buried too deep down by life
To a brief, magical space in time
When all the stars seemed to align
And flowers took on sacred shades
Under the glowing, gleaming bloom
The power of the mystic enduring moon.

## LOVE IS THE GREATEST GIFT

Love is the greatest gift.
Love's the most wonderful gift.
Only sweet love
Yes, only sweet love
Will enable my sweet soul to lift!

# LOVE, LIVE AND LEARN HOW TO FLY

Love, live and don't be afraid.
Life is the stuff
From which dreams are made.
Love is the key
To the door of the brave.
Love, live and don't be afraid.

Although this good life is tough
And it deals some bitter blows
It's the stuff what makes us us
And the way the sweet wind blows
And love glows
Throughout the valleys
And it blows throughout the hilltops
And it shows in the sweet sunshine
And resounds around the mountain
And it bristles in the city
Like electrifying lightening
And it blows away the cobwebs
Of the unconvincing frightening
And it grows
Within our very souls
As they achieve their heightening
And I smile, as I know
That love will conquer all
It will cause fears to fall
Love will rescue us all.

Yes – I'll love, live and not be afraid
For this life is the thing…
(and I *will* start to sing
and I *will* venture out
and I *will* dance and shout)
Yes – my life is the thing
From which dreams are made
I will love, live and not be afraid.

Love, live and learn how to fly
For love is the key between you and I
And love is the catalyst to spark us to fly
Yes, love is the secret to soaring on high.
Like a bird
At the dawn
Of a gold, silver morn
As us folks carry on
She bestows us with song
And we smile
As we hear
Her clear, harmonic notes
And we notice the breeze
Upon which her song floats…
Love will raise us to heights
We had never conceived
It will strong nurture might
To allow us to breathe
And to reach for the stars
And to bask in the sun
And relinquish the fears
That had caused us to run.

I will love, live and not be afraid
Yes! Life is the stuff from which dreams are made
And Love is the key to the door of the brave
I will love, live and not be afraid.

I will love, live and learn how to fly
I will reach for the sky
And my soul will soar high
I will swim to the sun
As my new life begins
As I soar through sweet light
I can fly
I'm in flight!

# LOVE ROSE

Love Rose
She burst through ground
Erupting as a tender, newborn shoot
She started, shy above the soil
Who housed her young yet ready heart
She grew as emerald green condensed around her path
Surrounding her with care and curling now
To house anew her growth
Into the tingling, breath-held air.

She grew, grew taller, still
A shoot of green magnificence
A sensual shining heart in waiting
All the garden contemplating
Licking lips anticipating maiden fair
To grace their sacred place
With presence, oh so magical, divine
The spellbound song of legend
As they waited and she, humble
Leaf by leaf prepared to shine.

And then - a bud appeared one day
Like a fleeting glimpse of unicorn
Unsure, the eyes, at sight between the trees
And as they held their breath still
As the greenery still breathed
Her heart, it heaved
Still wrapped in emerald cotton bud
Still safe from elements above
And as she waited in her mother's nurture womb
The dragonflies began to dance as one
They swirled the air and showered kisses
On her chosen spot to shine
The song of wings reminded her that time –
Her time to shine was nigh.

Next day, and showing now
Her red between the bud-lipped leaves
With a flash of flesh, of blood she teased
And as the garden celebrated
Her colour emanated passion
Sang soft song of revolution
Growing surer now that time was due
For her to bloom and shine.

And then that night
As moon shone down
And dewdrops tender placed themselves around
Anointed maiden, one, with sparkling spell
To coax the waiting princess from her shell
It whispered comfort
Reassured that yes!
Her star was set to shine
And as the miracle combined
The garden, all the flowers and bees joined hands
They formed a glowing circle
Sacred circle in support of the new queen
And as she breathed
Our Rose began to feel the sense
All senses swirling red with radiance
She took a breath and gathered confidence
And waited for the promise of the dawn
When Rose, she knew, life would anew begin.

And then that morning
Sent from heaven
Chirping birds alerted all the waiting world
To the miracle occurring
As magnificent and ready
Heaving heart with petalled passion
Rose, she soft as thunder breaking through the clouds
Began to open
And the velvet revolution
Life and fire and blood and evolution
So the shoot and bud they manifested
Treasure curled no more within their palm
Her growth now broken forth
Like a firework bursting rainbow
Shooting star of love, red love
Against the gleaming emerald grass
And as she celebrated living
Giving thanks with joyful colour
So love rose upon the hour
And the garden, overjoyed with love
It sang and danced before her.

## LOVE - YOU WILL SURVIVE

Do not hold your head so heavy
Do not clothe your heart in fear
Don't let worry cloud your judgement
Do not close your eyes and ears.

Do not cry such tears of sadness
Do not let them drag you down
Do not let your sweet soul sink low
Don't forget you're not alone.

Love – you hold the magic in you
Love – you hold the key to life
Love – your soul shines brightly through you
Love – and Love – you will survive.

MEMORY

Is every haunted, shame-filled sigh
To echo grief for time gone by?
Past memories of friends forgot
And nothing is, but what is not.

You saunter down ole mem'ry lane,
Attempt to dirge it up again;
Yet this 'nostalgia' eats away
The remnants of your Summer's day.

Those ghostly days for which you yearn,
The awesome stars which used to burn,
The flowered rows of times gone by –
An empty vase for which you cry.

From buried lands no joy will grow
Yet still you dream, because you know
That though you mourn each happy year
Where all is lost, I still am here.

Step out a while from pity's bliss
Say nothing, just hear me say this:
Ignore the life which lies ahead –
In doing so, you join the dead.

## MONEY DOESN'T MATTER

Money doesn't matter –
Are you still alive?
Money doesn't matter –
Can you laugh and breathe?
Money comes and money goes
All part of an elaborate show
To keep us from the truth we know –
That money doesn't matter.

Why should such a piece of paper
Make us lose our smiles and sleep?
Why should cold and dirty coinage
From our hopes and dreams us keep?
Does more money buy you peace?
Does more money buy you love?
Does more money make the sun shine
Brighter from the skies above?

Does more money make you nicer?
Does it make them love you more?
If it does – a gentle question:
What ya with these people for?

Does more money buy the future?
Does it make you kind and wise?
Does more money make your soul grow?
Does it open up your eyes?

Money comes and twists the brain
Money turns our lives insane
Money does not heal our pain
Money's just a lying game.

Modern man's obsessed with objects
Modern man's defined by greed
When distracted by our wanting
We forget the things we need.

Money doesn't matter
In love – not banks - I trust.
Being free of money matters
Is, my friends, a must.

Money doesn't matter –
Are you still alive?
Money doesn't matter –
Can you laugh and breathe?
Money comes and money goes
All part of an elaborate show
To keep us from the truth we know –
That money doesn't matter.

## MOTHER EARTH

Mother Earth
You breathe with me
I breathe with you
Oh Mother Earth.
I cannot comprehend your gift
This gift of such enormity
You give to me, to one and all
With all your wondrous worth.
Oh Mother Earth
Conceived not I
A circle oh so perfect.
Your pulsing, living sphere abound
With light and colour, joy and sound.
And dreamed not I before this time
Of such lush living lands combined
Entwined in perfect harmony
Of wind and mountain, soil and rain
And forest, flower and sea.
Oh Mother Earth
Magnanimous
Magnificent, so humble still
You seek not glory, no, nor recompense
For all we take – we take at your expense.
Oh Mother!
Truly Mother Earth you be,
Such silent giving love for all
And children, we,
I pray that soon will see
That as you give your love and care to us,
We must in turn, our love and care
Give back – give back to thee.
Oh Mother Earth!
I feel your pain!
The pain of ages – too long blind these souls
Who tread upon your shining surface
Ravage deep your cavernous womb
And pillage you for diamond, oil and coal.
Oh Mother Earth!
Forgive us please
That even one, one child of yours could steal
From your eternal purse of riches
Rape your lands and trawl your beaches
Cut your breathing, bounteous lungs to shreds
Where forests grew – now oil flows black instead.
I cry for you
Oh Mother Earth,
I cry your tears for you.
That we could show such hideous contempt
Or, arrogant, make any child exempt
From such great bounty you provide
Abundant wealth to nurture every child
Of yours, all equal in your eyes
Oh tender Mother dear
You hold no favoured ones
But love us in equality
Each face that skips upon your breast
Each child that basks beneath your sun
You hold no child the special one
But all we are, one child to you in love
One child upon your shining soil
One child so blessed by all the stars above.
I pray, oh Mother Earth, that we
Combine and start to shine together
As the billion droplets in the endless flowing sea
I pray that we
We move together now
To right the wrongs that somehow we have done
To you, to one, to all, our other, equal ones
That we reverse
The sorry curse
That fell so long like shadows on your plains
And start to put things right again
That finally
We wake up now
Now strikes the hour
The time long due.
Oh Mother Earth!
Please give us power
Please shower humility and love still more
That we can cleanse your aching shores
Reverse the rivers running black with oil
And purge the tainted from your shaking soil
And plant new seeds in dusty plains
That flowers and fruits and trees
May raise their bounteous heads again
And let us once more dance
On gleaming emerald grass
Beneath pure drops of fresh clean sparkling rain.
Let mountains move!
Oh Mother Earth!
And let your children prove our worth!
Let us start to love anew
Let new growth spring and crystal fountains flow
Let forests rise, horizon proud once more
And let us love you to your very core.
Let seas run deep and fish jump lush in love
And let soft puffball clouds once more
Rain only life and healing from above.
Let the deserts calm
Let your children raise their arms in peace
Bless us with your Godly, Goddess grace
Let us kiss your newly smiling face
And every fresh brave step we take
A move towards a brighter future make
That every blessed child of yours
Once more will live in harmony
Oh Mother Earth!
Please let it be!
And let a mother just like you
Step forth
From such a child as me.

## MUSE

Keep reaching for your muse
For she is all around you
As life's events confound you
To shock, delay, astound you…
Your muse may be a rose
Whose sweet perfume surrounds you
Whose petals lend
A splash of red
Adding drama to the bed
And vines stretch high
Into blue sky
They reach your head and crown you.

Your muse may be an eagle
Soaring high above you
Who from the sky protects, respects
As surely as she guides you.
And she will help you fly
As your direction finds you
From up above
She showers love
Sweet comforts to remind you.

A tree erupting from the ground
Breathing air and life abound
Whose fruitful branches lend you shade
A watcher giving accolade
A witness to your dawn begun
Most beautiful companion.
A butterfly, a buzzing bee
The first shoot of a foxglove leaf
The friend who helps you help you to achieve –
Whose love ensures you still believe.

## MUM AND DAD

How could I ever
Write a piece
To tell you
What you mean to me?
Words can fail
A humble poet
Speaking of
Her greatest mentors.
Where to start?
To start with picnic baby days
And knitted home-made smocks
And blankets spread upon the grass
To keep pure white
Those hand-made ankle socks.
Then waiting in the late day Summer Sun
For Dad to come back home from work
The bathing costumes ready packed
And simple sandwiches of jam
To feed him tea
While at the wheel
To take us where
The sun and sand revealed
The rock pools
Searching deep with Mum
We hunted for the crabs
And shells
And seaweed, barnacles and more
Starfish dancing across the rock pool floor.
And then the races
Ran with Dad
Jumping up to touch the leaves
And throwing sticks
Towards the skies
To liberate the conkers
From the great old mighty trees.
The love and joy!
The celebration!
Bursting life of family
The teaching, growing
Learning, flowing
Wrapped in love
Our little triangle of three.
Llansteffan sunshine
Walking barefoot in the village

Sunrise swims
To welcome in
The day with grace
And laughing, joyful
Thankful wave-dance
Morning dawning fresh new face
We raised the skies
With singing, chirping with the crickets
Walking wet back up the copse
Still the childhood barefoot freedom
Striding to
The local bread and butcher's shops
To make our sandwiches for breakfast
Appetite straight from the sea
And then to see
What else the day
Would serve us as in love we made our way.
The BBQs upon the beach
With cousins, mothers and their broods
With Gran's flat frying pan we rendered
Stomach filling
Steaming hot soul food
After Mum had lit the firewood
We'd all gathered
Traipsing through the sticks
We sat together
On the red rocks
Waiting in anticipation
Licking our expectant lips.
And then the castles!
How we built them!
Empires stretching across the sand
Adorned with flying flags and shells
Moats and bridges
Rivers running softly through them
Harmony with Mother Earth
Then waiting as the tide came in
And filled those moats
Until they overflowed.
Learning how to throw the discus
Taught by Dad
With large and flat round stones
Follow through
As you release
With fingertips –
The athlete's tips –
Then see them fly into the sea

With a plop!
Of self discovery!
Us three skimming stones
Upon the rivers
Counting how many jumps they made
Those stones, they seemed to skip for-ever
Then merge as one
Into the flowing everglade.

Memories
So strong, so sweet
Imprinted forever
On our eternal breeze.
I could go on
But feel this song
An epic could become
With memories
So filled with love
So wonderful and long.

How by Heaven
Did I find you
Swirling through this Universe of ours?
As then my ready renewed soul
Floated soft between the stars
Searching for the perfect place
To set my anchor
Call my home
My own
My life
My ours.

They say a child
Will choose her parents
Choose whose lives
To bless with hers.
It must be true –
This I believe
Because I know
That in this go
No others would I choose
But you
For you were made
To set me free
And I was made
To fly
With you.

## MY BEST FRIEND'S KITCHEN

In my best friend's kitchen
The world is put to right.
The strong, pure glow
As senses swell
Enveloped by the cooking smell
Eggs line up ready in their shells
As sundial plates
Sit on the shelves.
We reaffirm our very selves
In my best friend's kitchen.

In my best friend's kitchen
We sing out our true song.
We belt it loud
Together proud
We stand and laugh the day along
And garlic cloves, they wobble ready
Waiting for the heady twins
To cease our singsong for a moment
So some sweet cooking can begin.

And in the day
The children play
They pause to chitchat along the way
And teach us a thing or two, we'd say
We all meander throughout our day
And music rings
We jive and groove
Two strong soul sisters in the mood
With our gorgeous little dancing brood
So full of life, just overjoyed
We dance off all the sweet soul food
We'd earlier with love devoured.

And shells adorn the cwtchy corner
Stones and bark, essential oils
The candle pile, the driftwood shapes
The butterflies dancing
Along the walls
And frankincense imbues the air
As angels hover overhead
And sun shines down
Whatever the time
To bless
The sacred
Words that are said.

And on that table
Oh! The work!
The passion, love
The toil and care
As one soul paints, creates and sings
The other writes her poems there...
Philosophies
To put things right
And ease some suffering in the world
As one might expect –
The artists' rant –
That age-old revolutionary slant
"We'd make such a difference
If given the chance"
So go their soulful witchly chants...
And once in a while
With a sweet, knowing smile
They even some rich red wine decant.

The glowing orbs sway in the light
They show and play their souls' delight
Then as eve falls and slides to night
Warm sun becomes strong candlelight
We sit with open eyes soul wide
And move the orbs just with our mind.
There's magic of a special kind
In my best friend's kitchen.

## MY HUMAN RIGHT

To be free
Is what I was born for.
I was born for it
As I live for it.
To be me
Surely
Is the least I should ask for -
To expect and demand
My inherent right
To freely reflect my inner light
Or shout out
My brightest thought.
I cannot be bought.
My voice
Cannot be tamed or taught;
As my soul is aflame
So she will speak
She will sound
And she will stand her ground
And look you in the eye.
Oh! Hark my pure sweet song!
This joyful soul of mine
Will live on
Long after these prison bars have gone.
My personal ID card
Is the unique essence of my heart.
My right in this life
That was given to me
Is simply my right
To be free
To be me.

## MY PARTICULAR PART TO PLAY

My particular part to play at this instance in this time
During the rich mystical tapestry of this sacred life of mine
Is as poet and creator, muse and messenger divine
And with humble thanks I say, as the holy harpists play
And the rainbows radiate their warmth to illuminate the way
And the shadows part, as glowing heart emits her shining violet light
And sunrise burns, hot orange golden days aflame with fire's delight
The pen! The sword of peace and love, the arrow aiming, soaring true
To make love's mark, a firework start, combusting truth with mystic might;
'Tis granted that a poet's heart, so charged with passion to the truth impart
May speak in service to the one who asks for help to heal or lift their heart
Or hearts of others, or to honour life or love, or be in service to the light and love above.
As above so below. As the sunshine rays will glow. As the poet's soul will show.
And now by grace of mystic place of time and life and love and Mother Earth and space
Here, my heart, to you today imparted true with love and honourable intent:
An opportunity bestowed to me, to one, to you and all – this gift 'tis Heaven sent.
The palm when crossed with faith and love, will find a meeting guided by the stars
This is my duty, this my gift and now, this precious gift is also yours.

## MY SPACE

Think I need
To carve myself
A tiny little corner.
A cwtchy little corner
In a small, small room.
A bright room filled with bookshelves
And a hundred star struck candles
And a fairy chandelier
Glowing gracefully above me
And upon the walls
So richly placed
And uplit by soft embers
Magic tapestries of mountains
And lush forests filled with bluebells
Where the sun casts shadows on the grass
As folks through life and daydreams pass
And as I watch
I smile, and ask
To bless me in my corner.

And from the speakers on the walls
As dusk begins and daylight falls
Emits the ethereal sound
Of a million male choir voices
Softly lulling me to wonder
If the truth is here or yonder
And if breaking out
Or staying put
Is the best one of my choices.

## MY SWEETEST GIFT

Not for a slightest
I would of dreamed of
Doing it before.
But then fate knocked on my door.

More softly, sweetly, gently
Than I could ever have imagined
Or ever can explain…

With a firm, steady hand
Inviting – charging me to understand
She grasped my quivering soul
And smiling,
Beckoned me through the open door
And led me
Into light
And rainbow coloured sky.

I want to ask "How me?"
But can hardly bear
To ask –
I am so blessed –
Dare not assume
I have the right
To ask
About this kiss of bliss
Of sudden
Bursting
Reassuring joy
So thunderbolt struck into my heart
Never to be departed from again
Come sun, or beauteous rain.

This all-consuming love
Showered down from shooting stars above;
A glow
So hazy, bright and warm
So warming for my soul
And for my dreams
I cannot speak or write of it –
Only bask in and surrender to
The might of it.

And arms wrapped all around me –
The sound of silent, constant song
And joy of knowing
That I do belong.

How did such a soul as I deserve it?
Yet
Belief from out and in –
That's what happy state my soul is in!

And so
As I continue to grow
And grin
In the moment
Dance in the moonlight
And thank the universe
For this wondrous delight…

I light
Just one more candle
And turn
To learn
To pray
(and smile
and sing)
And reaffirm the beautiful –
The fundamental thread of things.

## MYSTIC SPIRIT

Mystic spirit seeps and spills
Enveloping the silent hills
Whispering through woods and dales
Captivating resting vales
Moving to the moonlight's call
As rays from parted clouds shine down
Seeking out the souls who seek
While the magic grasps them all;
Peaceful dwellers slumber deep
As the energies combine
Engulfing dreamers as they sleep
Caressing fingers touch and twine
Promising to secrets keep
When upon the dawn they wake
But for now they're unaware
Slumbering in velvet black.

## NEIGHBOURS

Neighbours are a funny breed
Whether the same
Or different creed.

An amazingly different world exists
The other side
Of the concrete wall
You know, they aren't like us at all -
They're not like us
Don't look the same
Don't talk or walk
Or shop the same
Don't even watch
The rugby game -
I don't know how they spend their time!

But then again, I have to say
The other day
When I went knocking
What transpired was really shocking
(Because I needed sweet brown sugar
To bake that chocolate cake for Father)
That door of theirs just opened...
Well!

I hardly could believe the smell!
Of perfumed spices
Saffron sweetness
Mellow herby chillied hotness
Honeyed notes
And flowered layers
Sticky toffee treacle warmness
Bay leaf scented
Thyme all dotted
Through with subtle hints of basil
Oregano
Mint and ginger
Thyme and pepper
Garlic heaven!

All these beauteous smells arising
From their glowing, cooking oven!

They even asked me
To take a seat
And offered up a generous
Plate so I could eat.

I had a bit
And I have to admit
That it really wasn't all that bad.

## NO

Turmoil turmoil aching through my blood
My bones and through my aching soul
Devastating realisation contemplation
To extend and stretch the horror films
Of nightmares beating hard and fast
Their heart beneath my heaving breast.
Not to ingest – Out. Out! I Say!
I tell you these horror films are not welcomed in my way.
Your blood it boils it bubbles, volcanoes break
And gush out loud their hurt, they cry
They roar upon unto the heavens in their anguish
Rivers break their banks and boulders crash
Come tumbling down from cliff-heads
Towering o'er the shaking sea
I fight the turmoil buried deep the shadow inside me.
It overcomes, I overcome.
Will not be done
Until this turmoil anguish breaks and flies away.
'Tis not for my heart.
I refuse its whispering baying.
No, No I stand here saying.
Say again and will say ever more.
This word.
No.
I give it to you now as it echoes through my core.

No.

No more.

## NOBODY CARES

Whilst sitting in the sunshine
I heard a shadow whisper
"Nothing, no-once cares
No-one cares about you."
It took me back a little bit
As shadowed words can do
And so I started to peruse
If this were really true.
I went outside to sit awhile
Connect fresh air with stagnant mind
And as I sat, began to find
The answers starting to unwind...

The bird that landed
On the fence
Began to sing such tender notes
She soothed my soul
And calmed my fears
And washed away those transient tears
With the beauty of her melodies.

And then
As straighter I began to sit
I saw a little spider
Weaving her web of silken fire
To catch the greedy greenfly feeder
Ready to desecrate my rose...
I thanked her for her awesome work
And left her to in peace compose.

And when I raised my head to sky
I saw a wondrous butterfly
She floated soft
On the sweet air...
And then a miracle occurred!
She landed softly on my nose
('tis big enough, I suppose!)
She whispered soft,
That only I could hear...
And what she said –
That butterfly?
She said:
"My child, I care".

I went inside
Now smiling wide
And thanking all my stars
And as I thanked them
They appeared
And twinkled even more.

## ODE TO A TOURIST

I live on the edge of paradise
I witness your pleasure and your vice
I see you rest beneath the sun
I hail your holiday begun
I hear you play beneath the palms
I watch you quash away your qualms
Of stressful times in the city
I choose to ignore your pity.
I imagine your delight each day
As the sunlight paves its way
Over the sands
Across our lands
Through mountain glades
Casting shades.
I watch your carefree children play
And dance away each hazy day
I feel you taste the sweet delight
Of tropical fruit-punch at night.
I want to rest and bathe and laugh
Beneath the sun
Throughout the grass
Over the sands
Behind the wind
Delighting in
All human kind.
I'm glad to see you feed the birds
The hunger here must not be heard
I hear you laugh your carefree joys
Bestow on you my country's muse.
I hope you sleep and rest with ease
Your heads beneath this gentle breeze
But most of all, do come again
So that this sweetness carries on.

ODE TO PELAGIA

Pelagia, Pelagia, how your golden curls frame face of peach
Sweet peach and cream, they blend upon the canvass
Of long ancient timeless lands - yet somehow out of reach
From where you stand - 'neath new times' thunder clouds,
Still - here you shine as maiden true; those sparkling eyes
They shine so soft and blue; as lashes brush and kiss
Your blushing cheeks a dewdrop settles in my mind's eye –
I, the poet see a drop adorn your lash like flashing diamond
Sparkles sad yet still, still future-sure, sweet calm beneath the rain;
It promises, my love, to set alight the fire in your sweet eyes again.

Pelagia, Pelagia, how your golden curls they sing your song
Of haystacks, harvest, ripe the pleasure, as old Autumn winds blew long
Into the easy, sun-filled eve, upon your Mother Earth you stood and breathed,
Your breasts, they heaved full bloom - and promised they to render
With their ample, giving, tender bosom, pleasure - and a gift
Of life you brought to grace your waiting, loving, endless arms
The babe, it cried, your heart it warmed, as soft and new in love it sang
And as you held her in your cradle, Heaven's stars appeared and shone
Oh Pelagia! How you did her proud, the babe she grew as shades grew long
Pelagia, how you stood so fearless, stood the tender mother tall and strong.

Pelagia, it is time now for your magic strides to tread once more
The boards of waiting stars in eyes and songs sung from above you
Deep within you, hear the roar of heart - your heart, she loving tells you
Soft she whispers message clear, for you, sweet golden child, for you to hear
She breathes the message on the waiting winds, imparts an arrow true
She flies through clouds and drifting stardust, sings to you a rhyme of times –
Those times past and the time now and those times still yet to come –
And as you stand beneath the sunlight and it highlights angel dust on golden curls;
Your future set so clear, so ready, set upon the path now to unfurl –
How I thank you Pelagia, for your magic kiss of love throughout the ages sang
So read these lines, sweet Pelagia, strong with faith to see your future life begin.

## OH FAIRY FORTRESS

Oh fairy fortress
Shining in the mystic night
Will you make my dreams come true tonight?
They are honest dreams
And just
Pretty fair I think
As fair as your fairest fair fairy facade is pretty…
Paying a compliment?
Moi?
But in all sweet seriousness
Bless us with your magic
And please pass your mighty magic on
But just to us of course!
Not to any foes!
(OK, I didn't need to tell you that
I take it back.)
As you smolder
In the moonlight
And quiver
In the river light
I shimmer
As you glimmer
With such a depth of delight…
Anticipation
For our great, humble nation.
You house dreams of children
And elders alike
Create brothers and sisters
Dreams, prayers and wishes
You make us forget our fears for a night
Or a day
And sometimes a couple of months even.
You truly are a fairy fortress
That with love alone has conquered
The strongest
The mightiest
The toughest
The roughest
There are and ever were.
Still shine
With tender passion and magic might
You've housed so many deeply noble fights.
And together
We really won them all
And still continue to win.
For we are here
Together
As one
For those brief beautiful moments
In heart and mind and soul
And common goal.

Yes, the charms you hold are famed throughout the globe.
You do have the magic power to turn coal dust into gold.
All due respect.
The legends must be true.
You must be pretty special.
You made me talk to a stadium.

## OH IN THE LONG WINDING BILLOWS OF MY MIND

Oh in the long winding billows of my mind
I find truth aches
It cataclysmic breaks
From solitude of being surrounded
Confounded, unfounded
Grounded fears
Of tears I fear to release.
The noose shakes
Upon the mistakes
Of its resurrection.
I have begun now
And at my soundless start
The architect of time
Ensured my watch was set to strike
Upon this hour
This waiting minute sleeping sure
And still
Until it came on
Bursting out
Around about and through
The pain we all go through –
This life.
But why wait
For the fate we contemplate
Can be a merry thing.
Our fate –
Should we not hesitate
Allow our souls to sing –
To ring out now?
The hour
Grows louder
Feeds
The holler
Beneath the collar
Of the clothes
That scream
For freedom.

## ONE AUGUST SUNDAY MORNING

Nothing flew and nothing moved
But a solitary bee.
The skies lay still – they'd had their fill
And the earth beneath them tried to breathe.
A butterfly lopped then gently stopped
Attop a still-born bud.
A single ant chased ghostly chants
Of comrades lost through cracks of mud.

The stillness grew – still nothing flew;
The waiting watchers frowned.
Then they as one – devoid of sun
In silence waited
Breath abated
Heavy, hazy, contemplated –
Braised their lungs with woeful songs
As in the air they drowned.

## OPEN

Open my eyes
That I may see.
Open my ears
That I may hear.
Open my heart
And remove all fear.
Give me my strength
And hold me near.

## PARALLEL WORLD

To contemplate a parallel world
And hold up the glass that we may see
Is to deny the value of a pearl
Our hidden gem
So intricately
Intimately, delicately
Encased, enshrouded by charade -
My prima donna of disguise,
Clear beauty hid by sheer facade
Designed to trick the mind and eyes.

To contemplate a parallel life -
The debauchery
Of self-torturey.

To bemoan 'why me'
Is never to see
The beauty and power
Of the world that is ours.

## PEACE

I ache for you
Break my heart for you
Shake to start for you
Would depart for you
Live my life for you
Suffer strife for you
As I wait for you
Knowing I must do
What I need to do
Showing faith in you
As we all must do.
You elusive come
As the shadows run
Whilst I wait my turn
Fires rage and burn
Then the daylight breaks
Blows away the fakes
Still left standing here
In awe of your allure
And the cure you hold
Precious more than gold
Warm as smiling sun
Calm as shining sea
Yes, you rest in me
Peace – please set me free.

## PERFECT

Be not ashamed
For you are perfect
As you are.

Be not afraid
More spirits than you know
Do care.

Be not disgraced
For you have grown
From those 'mistakes'.

Be not in hate
It is a fake
Illusory state.

Be not in guilt
For you have done
What you could do.

Be not alone
For angel souls
Surround you.

Be not ashamed
For you are perfect
As you are.

Love, if this were not so
You wouldn't be you
And you wouldn't be here.

## PROGRESS

The trick is in moving forwards.
Because we all
Just want to progress.
To move, grow
Expand, stand, flow
Digress...
Effervesce! Expect! Demand!
Reflect, project, invest, digest
Rest.
But yes.
Move forwards
Walk on
As life carries or strings us along
And we conceive and build
The ever-increasing
Converse pyramids
One for each shoulder
Insurmountable boulders
Our great expectations
Expected, collected,
Success on successes
I am when I posses this –
As the eyes and nods of others
Bless the measure of my successes.
It should be easy. I want to get there.
But not to get *there.*
Just to achieve
Beyond the limits of my soul
To cry and love
To feel, to breathe
Without ever ceasing to believe
Or dream.
For life before me to unfold
With sunshine and fruit
And stories told
Family, friendship, tales of old
And hopes for a future
Filled with hazy light
Bright
Warm, busting with joy.
Aglow. Humble.
Simple.
I want to get *there.*
Simple and free
To pick the morning apple
From the tree
Crunch the shiny flesh
Let the tangy juice refresh
And pat the bough
Delight in now.
Appreciate
Relate
Elate!
Communicate with life
The world around me
My universe and apple tree
To live now
Love
To look around and up above
Into the eyes of the ones I love
Into the mirror
The eye of life
To face head on
To try
Head high
No – do!
I shout!
Without a doubt!
I'll drink all joys that life gives out
I'll sing, dance, laugh –
I'll live life now.

## PULSE

I feel the pulse of ebbing sands
I sense the grain run through my hands
Today, this day, I look within
While outside flows the constant grain
The time has come, as lands converge
And ice-sheets, mountains, rivers merge
As winds blow high and faults run deep
And humans rouse from waking sleep
The grain flows free, it soft runs down
My arms, my legs and gathers 'round
My feet, the sweet smell swirling through
My senses as an open door
I look ahead, the path extends
I liberated, drop my hands
My mind's eye wide I travel forth
Behind me standing gleaming door
I travel on with confidence
In light and love She guides my steps
In faith He keeps my rooted feet
Though tears of love my wide eyes weep
I know I grow each blessed step
I choose my way, decide my path
As thinner grows the matrix veil
I choose to elevate my soul.

## QUIETUDE

Quietude, I ache for you
I long for sunlit rippling lake
Ashining blue into the hush-filled breeze
As still the trees they contemplate
The soaring bird asurfing high on winds
Where only whispers of the Gods are heard
And rays of sunshine speak their gentle words
Through lazy shadows cast on sparkling emerald grass
That flutters in the moving of the swaying, lounging blades
Through the language of the wind and stars and sun and moon and shades...
And as I ask for peace and solace
In these beautiful surroundings
Sense a sense of love confounding
Ancient tears, as breeze and sun combine
To dry those past-pain waters on that aching, changing face of mine...
And as the tender sun still shines
Bestows a glow upon the surface
As the silver streaks they dance, the tune
It fills my heart so full, my senses calmed to overflowing...
Oh, sweet quietude,
I find you in the resting corner of my heart
Depart all else, all noise, distraction, doubt
And only truth to me impart
Oh! Lovely quietude I find you
Waiting, glistening within me
Deep in soul, in heart, in spirit,
Nestling in singing solitude
Oh! Quietude, sweet quietude
You're here!
Now found, you fill my soul
With never-ending peace and love
And calm and warmth and gratitude.

## REINCARNATION

The
Reincarnation
Of
A
Mother's
Dreams
Is
To
See
Her
Daughter's
Light
Shining
In
Her
Eyes.

## RISE UP THE GODS

Rise up the Gods!
Your calling dawns
Yesterday
The hour was near
Appeared still brighter
Ever closer
Hour by hour
Today
'Tis here.
Rise up your arms!
They burst with strength
And peace
And wisdom
Hot to touch
Enough!
They hold
The power within them
Humble singing
Passion raging.
Rise up in peace!
To shine among us
Lend us your strength
And bring us close
As this
The dawn
Of the hour
Appears here
Rise up the Gods!
This day, you've stayed for!

## SEASON'S BLESSINGS

Love and light and peaceful wishes
Joy-filled days and sunshine kisses
Ring the bells of look within you
Feel the truth that rests within you.

As the pine scent wraps around you
Feel the glow of candles burning
Live – embrace your sweet soul's burning
Be at one with your soul's yearning.

As the wine flows, as the nuts crack
Givers give – give of your soul back
Give to live, bestow your light back
Praise this grace to give and give thanks.

As the sun sits, rests in splendour
Stills three days in waiting wonder
As she burns still focus yonder
Nod to past time, look beyond her.

Feel your vision, see you deeply
Feel supremely, see you clearly
Sense abound, deep light, sweet sound
Your angels singing all around;

Hands outstretched, it's yours to take them
Shake your soul to singing, freedom
Blink your eyes to finding, seeing
Look within, be beyond being.

Feel each blessing, dance each daybreak
Sing to sun your soul's sweet namesake
Give thanks for your deepest heartache
Feel your spirit from its shell wake.

This, the time to look within you
See the past you, move beyond you
Give with love as lovers can do
Love your others, love the one you.

Love each pine cone, love each petal
Love your sisters, brothers, angels
Love the dawn, each light's new favours
Love this life – it's yours to savour.

## SHINE

Shine, beautiful
Exude your light and spirit
Be not afraid
Life wills you to live it
To grasp with both hands
And mighty effort
Not to shrink, but grow
Swell, move
Flow
Expand
Demand the light
Reflect it
Reflect upon it
Do with it as your heart leads you
Be true to it as your soul pleads you
Never dismiss
The kiss
Of a sunbeam
The dawn
Of your life's dream
The need
Of a primeval scream
To shine
Divine
Just shine.

UNITED ARTISTS

## SHOUT!

Shout Love!
Peace!
Freedom!
Believe!

Shout life
Stands
Ahead
Of me!

Shout
Trust In lovers!
Love my brothers!
Swing with my sisters!
Love all my others!

Shout sing for sweet freedom!
Shout joy for each nation!
Shout life's celebration!
Shout pure exaltation!

Shout knowledge is power!
Shout faith in each other!
Shout honour thy mother!
Shout love like no other!

Shout trust and compassion!
Shout feeling and action!
Shout sweet education!
Shout soul satisfaction!

Shout shining together!
Shout loving forever!
Shout life is for living!
Shout soaring to Heaven!

Shout Love!
Peace!
Freedom!
Believe!

Shout life
Stands
Ahead
Of me!

Shout trust in lovers!
Shout faith in each other!
Shout love like no other!
Shout shining together!

## SIDE BY SIDE

Mother Nature
As every day awakes
And fades
Appreciates
Our differences
She celebrates the constancy
Of so many colours
And roots rooted
Together
Born of many climes
Over ages
And journeys
Now joined
Survival stories combined.
Living in the same soil
Sharing the sweet air
Nourished side by side.
Not blind,
She doesn't mind
Nor discriminate
Or comprehend how to hate
But allows each bud
Space
Time to grow
To grace
The land
One equal race
Sharing, giving, living
Accommodating
Ingratiating
One with every other
With sisters and brothers
Our others
In our communal space.
Mother Nature doesn't choose who to shine on.
She loves every face.

## SING

Where are the Welsh
Voices
Rising from the valleys?
I can't hear them loud enough today
If at all.

Sing
People of Wales.
It's what they know us for.
It's the only thing that they expect
But we don't deliver
Anymore.

Are we really such a silent people?
My Gran's gossip coffee morning
Tells me different.

So did the miners.
Singing their way
To their joyous
Daily toil.
It was tough work, but it was theirs.
They sand as they ground
The black gold dust
From beneath the sacred, gracious hills.
They sang out
Their rights in the commons.
For their common kindred.

But She
Stopped them.

And the rest was silence.

Those ones I knew
Weren't ones to lay down and die.
But those days are gone now –
Today
It's you and I.

Now it's time
To relight and reignite
The ghosts of coal burning fires
Around which the family gathered
And were safe.

It's a disgrace
That the strong pure voices
Of our heritage
Our proud ancestors
Are now vanished from that lovely place.

We owe it to our Fathers
And to their old lands.
May the old language live on...
Yet us Welsh of today barely whisper
Our words
Let alone
Belt out our song.

Tarnished?
Broken?

Owain and Llewellyn
Would never lay down and surrender
Or even train themselves
To understand the meaning of those words.

They still lie in wait
For our call.
But it doesn't come.

Sing.

People of Wales.

A new era of ours
Is long overdue
To be begun.

## SLEEP, SWEET CHILD

Sleep, sweet child
And have sweet dreams.
Tomorrow's a world away
It seems
You'll rise up fresh
And wake anew
To smile ahead
At pastures new.

Some say that when
A child starts dreaming
The elves and fairies
Start believing
And come out from their magic homes
To soft upon the planet roam...

They kiss the sleeping child in bed
They hold her hand
Caress his head
So when that child
Awakes at dawn
They're filled with love
To carry on.

So, sleep, sweet child
And have sweet dreams.
Tomorrow's a world away
It seems
You'll rise up fresh
And wake anew
To smile ahead
At pastures new.

99% ANGEL

## SMILE

So sweet!
So unexpected!

The burst of joy that comes
When you meet another one –
Come together with a passing soul
On the street
Along your path in life
For a magical, momentary respite
From the stress of getting
Somewhere
To do
Something
You don't want to do anyway.

But to see
Another soul
With a smile
On the way
Makes your day!

How I dream of a simple and beautiful world
(A bit like it was just a little while ago)
Where we smile at each friend
That we pass on the street
And look straight in their eyes
As we each say "Hello!"

## SOMEONE

Someone's always there
My dear
Someone's always there.
No matter what life throws at you
Someone always cares.
Life can be a lonely place
It wears so thin our worldly face
And in the place of glowing soul
We cry and clothe ourselves in cold
Our shoulders weighted with disgrace
And grief and pain etched on our face.
But even through
Those darkest days
When kind compassion
Stays
Away
I can with joy and comfort say
That Someone's always there.

We weren't put on this shining earth
To hide away and beg for mercy
Our job is to stand tall
And shine
To strong join hands
Yet sing as one.
And even when it really feels
That no one's at your side
That gaping hole surrounds your soul
And stretches far and wide;
Do not give up
And don't despair
My sweet,
You're not alone.
Yes, Someone's always there
My love
To listen to your song.

That soul may be in front of you
Or living just next door
Or just a thousand miles away
But close enough to care
Or they may be
The glowing soul
Who down from Heaven stares...
And showers kisses on your head
And tucks you up in cosy bed
And always will be at your side
To hold your hand and ease your mind
And who will always love bestow
(That's yours to keep and yours to know).

Yes, Someone's looking after you
And Someone's watching over you
And Someone loves you cos you're you
And Someone hopes you love them too.

So take these words
And hold them tight
And when you rest your head tonight
Remember
Someone's always there
And
Someone
Always
Cares.

## SOMETIMES WE CAN FEEL SO SMALL

Sometimes we can feel so small
When dark shadows upon us fall
Standing helpless at the helm
Before an overwhelming realm
Cowering and overcome
Kneeling at the kingdom come
And over us the tower tall
Threatens to upon us fall
Intimidates with majesty
Defies our mind, confines beliefs.
Sometimes we can feel so low
When strength and grandeur others show
And we crouch helpless down below
Trembling to let it out
To cowed to shout
Or voice defiance
Conquered by our mild compliance.
Sometimes we can feel so small
Sometimes we can feel so low
When our confidence has left us
We forget how life has blessed us.
Like the stony castle keep
The grand facade
That fools and guards
That fights to hide its own fears deep
We must our souls in courage steep
We must be bold and courage show
And stand our ground for what we know.

## SSHHHH

Hush hush
Rush rush
Mind bending
Right amending
Night acquiring
Light denying
Moral stretching
Conscience vexing
Mind perplexing
Soul convexing
Never ending
It's exhausting
Got
To tell
The Secret.

## STAND BEHIND A WATERFALL

Stand behind a waterfall
To see the world through different eyes.
Listen to your instinct call
And filter out the thin disguise
Of what you see and what you hear
As day to day you move through life
For what you see may not be true
And even less of what you hear.
Just let the drops refresh your skin
Feel the water, look within
Look beyond
Ignore the pull
Of common sense
And senses lulled
It's just a game
It's not all true
This fragile world
Revolves and fools...

And when you hear the water's noise
Drowning out the outside din
When you let the droplets haze
Your normal vision, look within.
You must upon yourself rely
For only you feel what you know
And on the trusted folks held dear
(Whose trust is certain – hold them near)
When you possess a different means
Of looking out upon the scene
When you can use this vital gift
The haze before your eyes will lift
When you can set your instinct free
Then you will realise your dreams
Just stand behind a waterfall
And listen to your instinct call.

## STAND UP BEAUTIFUL

Stand up, Beautiful
And raise your lovely head
You can lift your spirit high
While lying in your bed
You can set the sun alight
And you can find your inner might
And you do know that it is right
To let your spirit soar.

Stand tall, Beautiful
And raise your face to Her
She derives her energy
From the sweet smile you wear
She is with you all the while
Love is with you, laugh and smile
Though the physical beguiles
Life still shines through you.

Reach high, Beautiful
God is at your side
In whatever form He takes
Or She – you will decide
To reach for light
And let in love
And thank the sky, sun, stars above
For as you grow
You'll come to know
That God is in you too.

## STRONG

Strong – Be strong.
When all your strength has left you
This love will not forget you
This heart will always bless you.

Strong – Be strong.
This life is just a challenge
A gift disguised as madness
With steps to make us stronger.

Strong – So strong
You are to still be here, dear
You've been to make it through, dear
With all you've had to do dear.

Strong – So strong!
You rose to every challenge
You strode o'er every mountain
You drank from life's pure fountain.

Strong – Live long.
Your time to struggle's over
The past's behind your shoulder
No longer needs to hold you.

Strong – Be free now.
Your life is there inside you
Your friends are here to guide you
Your angels to remind you.

Strong – We love you.
We send you joy and sunlight
We send you the eternal light
We send you peace and lend our might
We give you strength and hold you tight
We promise it will be alright
We'll keep you through the darkest night
And clouds will part to shine the light.
Just still be strong
And smile along
Though life is tough
Still sing your song
You'll make it
As you've always done
Yes darling,
Still be strong.

## SUMMER IS THE TIME FOR LOVE

Summer is the time for love
Time to bask in yellow light
Amber, orange, pink she glows
Summer's twilights where love grows
Dusky dreams and breathless days
Laughter, life, the languid laze
To see each other's eyes
And gaze
To be amazed
And overcome
To let your senses overrun
To free your soul
To fly
To reach
To share your dreams
To learn and teach.

We are all just butterflies
Like the couple on the grass
Green as lime and lush as love
On cushioned air they float above
The smiling daisies far below
Kindred souls who share
Who know
The glow
The joy
The key to life –
To look into each others' eyes.

As the birds who sing along
The couple joined in soul and song;
As the dazzling dragonfly
Darting, shining by their side;
With the light and life she brings
Flowered fields and birds who sing;
As Summer shines her newborn sun
So she shines on love begun.

## SUNSHINE MISTS

Sunshine mists astretch the sky
Green grass grows long, vast clouds roll by
And spirits raise their faces high
Ask why they stand here now.

The rolling hills stay tall in wait
The birdsong stills and glades retreat
Soft silvered mirrored lakes reflect
And spirits stand in circumspect.

Dense forests raise to brush the blue
The gusts of wind send ripples through
The bluebells hush deep down below
And foxes howl as if they know.

Then with the dawn the silence breaks
As golds and pinks and reds ignite
And sunshine wins her daily fight,
Sweet souls stand strong prepared for flight.

## SURVIVAL OF THE FITTEST

Kiss me baby
As we float around
Alone in our worlds
Together in our world.
Our lake of peace
And threats.
The horizon blooms
It glows and beckons
It is uncertain
But filled
With warm possibilities
And hazy hope
Of chance encounters
Futile connectivity
And survival of the fittest
Or those who love the most.

SWEET BEE FLY FREE

Carefree bee
Buzzing free
Were I thee
Fly wth glee
Laugh for joy
Flower to flower
Gathering pollen
By the hour
Task so solemn
Honey maker
Flower grower
Colour shower
Life creator
Loyal fighter
Sight delighter
Seed igniter
Stem to petal
Heavy metal
Muse for music
Friend of tulips
Life defender
True contender
Nature's essence
Effervescence!
Reminder of life
Provider of food
Lifter of moods
Queen of the brood!
Magnificent
Significant
Nectar giver
Sweet deliverer
Intent
God sent
Sweet bee
Fly free
Safe from hands of man like me.

## SYNCHRONICITY

Synchronicity – it bursts
As rainbow born of sun and rain
Epiphany through joy and pain
To arch her way through clouded sky
Remind that hope and change is nigh
And as we sigh, eyes freshly wide
We leave the pain and past behind
As coloured arc becomes our guide
Sweet miracles still more we'll find.

Synchronicity – it swims
As fish a'leaping from a star-set lake
Reminding us in contemplation
All us children of creation
Yes! A chance in life to take
As leaping fish, our dreams we'll make
When only we, as fish so free
Will take that flying leap of faith
Then sweet rewards we'll start to see.

Synchronicity – it flies
Whilst kneeling still we contemplate the wild
We sigh as nature's lovelorn child
Then through the breeze
A magic winged thing appears
And dragonfly lands nearby
As gift appearing from the sky
Reminds that change is due and near
Reminds how fruitless were our fears.

Synchronicity – it laughs
As baby's eyes that search for truth
Once found, she raises head to skies
And laughs sweet peals of golden light
Reminds that life is beautiful
And as a laugh in silent room
Or as a single rose in bloom
That joy will shine through stagnant gloom
And sun will shine through darkest night.

Synchronicity – it wows
As lightning bolt from thunderous clouds
Though black they hover overhead
And shadows cast on flower beds
Yet when the magic moment's right
Electrifying nature's might
Will flash a gleaming sword of light
Reminds, the striking lightning fork
That light is there to shine through dark.

Synchronicity – it flows
As river running deep below
The surfaced world on which we tread
Thinking not with heart, but head
Yet still she runs, she gleams and flows
Until it reaches time to show
Then bursts through ground as crystal stream
Appears before us as we dream –
Reminds all is not as it seems.

## THANK YOU

Even when
The dark clouds loom
And rain pelts down
And cold winds blow
Still I know
The sun will show
And flowers will grow
And love will glow.

For this comfort
For this light
For this truth
That deep I know
For the rain
And for the sun
And for this love
I thank you so.

## THANK YOU FOR BEING IN MY LIFE

Mother, Father, Husband, Elder,
Sister, Brother, Friend and Neighbour
Child and Teacher
Cousin, Stranger
One Forever
Us Together.
Thank you
So much
For being in my life.

Your perfect cosmic timeliness
Amazes and gently delights
Each time you shine before me
Each time you shine your light
Always
Though sometimes our faces
Pass in silence
Love, respect
Yet knowing, always glowing, growing
Showing, each together
Always joined
In shining spirit
Shared in soul
Eternal company of hearts
Our heart
One heart
One goal
Departed all else
All remaining
Truth
One soul and perfect pathly timing
Never ending sweet combining
One star shining
Mighty gentle
Soft and strong
Unique blueprint of breath and life
Of love and laughter
Joy and song
This life
Our life
One Life
One Heaven
One Earth.

I thank you so much
For being in my life

## THANK YOU FOR BELIEVING

Thank you for believing
And thanks for believing in me.
Not everyone has the gift of sight,
Not everyone wants to see.
Not everyone wants to spend their time
To help another soul
Not everyone wants to shine their light
To show another the way to go.
Not everyone wants to expend their breath
To bestow their sweet advice;
Not everyone would spend that breath again
Or maybe even thrice.
Not everyone goes out of their way
For another person's gain,
Not everyone gathers comfort
In soothing another's pain.
Not everyone thinks that we are here
To make our way together
So thank you for believing in me,
I'll say thanks for your gift forever.

## THANK YOU FOR THE UNIVERSE

Thank you for the universe
And thank you for this life.
Thank you for the fellow souls
Who stand strong by my side.
Thank you for the miracle
Of everything on earth.
From every leaf
To sparkling seas
Each mother giving birth.
Thank you for the sunshine
That shines through my sweet soul
Thank you for the light inside
My candle, my eternal guide;
Thank you for the angels
Who nurture every stride
Who hold my hand
My heart expand
Are always at my side.
Thank you for each dewdrop
And each blade it's moisture holds.
Thank you for my body, mind,
My heart, my song, my soul.
Thank you for each dance I dance
Thank you for the music!
Thank you for this green, green grass
Thank you for the muses.
Thank you for my family
Those kindred lights who shine with me.
Thank you for the past and now
And thank you for the what will be.
Thank you for the mystery
Thank you for the joy of life!
Thank you for each thing I know
For every chance to learn and grow.

Thank you for each scented petal
Swaying in each coloured breeze;
Thank you for each butterfly
And every bird and every bee.
Thank you for the gift of wings
Thank you that my soul is free;
Thank you for the knowledge
That I exist to shine as me.
Thank you for the hurt and pain
Thank you for the suffering
Thank you for the clouds and rain
For each new day that shines again.
Thank you for the moon and sun
Thank you for the stars and sky
Thank you for the reasons why
Thank you for the questions!
Thank you for this winding path
And for my sweet decisions.
Thank you for each hour I wake
Thank you for each breath I breathe
Thank you for what I'll achieve
Thank you that I do believe.
One more sweet thing my soul must sing!
The greatest gift sent from above!
Thank you for the life affirming
Wonder making
Planet shaking
Dream creating
Celebrating
Synchronised by time vibrating
Sweetest gift that could be mine
My holy grail, the one divine
Thank you for the light that shines
Thank you for the Love.

## THE ANSWERS ARE BLOWING IN THE WIND

The answers are blowing in the wind
My friends
And the answers are glowing in our souls.
On the journey to find
The answers
For everything
The story is set to unfold...
We can't think our way
Out of this predicament
We can only
Feel our way
Towards
Personal fulfilment
As we bend
Towards the truth
And we seek out
Rays of light
As we try
To summon courage up
To make our peace, take flight.
As we try to find delight
Through our daily testing plights –
The answers are blowing in the wind.

Yes the answers are blowing
In the wondrous gentle wind
And the answers are showing
In our vast expansive minds.
This never ending story
Is set to unfold
And the answers are glowing
In the lovelight of our souls.

## THE COAL EXCHANGE

The Coal Exchange, The Coal Exchange
The coal-gold glowing soul of Wales
She harks me back to the finer days
Of the great Great Coal Exchange.
And dŵr was somehow purer then
And humankind was more your friend
And Cardiff city mix of faces
Went about their daily graces
Melting pot from hot and cold
Climes smiled together in the old
Times past when men were brothers –
Friends – and helped each other one make ends
Meet – meeting neighbours on the street – those strides
Such pride, delight to greet, to meet another one
Under the sun of the so sweet long ember days
In Wales – those days I knew in Wales.
And men
Exchanged their dragon blood
For meagre wage
Those fire-eyed haunted strong from churning toiling
Hardly saw the light yet saw it all through soot-lit
Soul knit sparkle carved starved blackened eyes
Except on weekend feast and rugby days
When all the laughing local lads and beauties, Mams and Dads
And Mam-gus Tad-cus, children, babies gathered
There to wile the wild Welsh day away
Sharing humble pies and telling stories of those 70's rugby glories
Plenty of them. Chests all puffed. Smiles. Chicken thighs.
Rhubarb blackberry tart.
Home-made gooseberry ice-cream
And a pint or three of Brains
(Though – Buckleys always was the one for me).
And so you see
My friend
The Great Great Coal Exchange
Lives on and on
As surely as she strived and cracked those whips of hers
Until we cried, it is the legacy of days,
It is the way the theatre plays –
It is our song.
Yes – The Great Coal Exchange lives on.
And now that song, to this sweet day still plays
It fills the bellows mellow with her mystic male-voiced gentle notes
Of no regrets and dragons' scarlet flying pride;
The fires of dragons dance, still dance inside
Still tread her boards, still handshake strong
Within her heart and with her soul and on her stage
They cry her song; within her time-held spellbound
God-sent sacred ground those souls belong.

## THE FIELD

I sit, surrounded by a field
A field so bright, so warm and sweet
It twinkles, moving to the soft enchanting breeze
Like lightly dreaming ballerinas swaying in their sleep
A million flowerheads swooning, dancing
Butterflies float overhead
A starlight, crystal bud appearing
Bursting through the eternal flower bed
And song – so soft, a lullaby of sorts
With notes of honey, petal wind chime tingling
Fairies singing, fireflies glowing,
Moon unveiling, starry, wondrous sky appearing
Lovers hand in hand delighting
Firework misted dawn igniting
Sunshine breaking through the grass
To cast a spotlight on each dewdrop
Shining each, a world unto their glowing universe.

## THE GOLD ACROSS THE RIVER

The gold across the river
Glimmers
It shivers, quivers
Flickers
Beckons
Invites
Delights
Castrates.

It gives off the aura
Of all that is called for
But all I don't have.
I'm a Chav.

It makes me believe
My tired eyes could deceive
Makes me think
I must be mad.

I know I should be glad
Of my lot
But I'm not.
And it shows.
I briefly wonder why
And start to cry.

Oh golden glimmer
You make me quiver
And shake and ache.
When will I wake?
My mortal peace is at stake!

As my heart breaks
My progress waits
And the green green grass
Keeps growing fast
Right beneath my feet.

THE KEY

I've travelled this earth
Over aeons
Through years
Searching for the key.
Examined this life
And questioned my mind
To seek the truth in me.

I've stretched out my hands
'Cross a million lands
To with this earth connect.
I've introspected
Hours and months
Held the mighty mirror in my hands
Reflecting the glistening whitening
Of the light
And my enlightening.

And in the beginning
The key I found
Was always in my hands
And rainbow that I searched for
Ended at my feet.

# THE LIGHT WILL SHINE AGAIN

Life
Like a volcano erupts
And thrusts us to the ground
Without a sound
Or with a mighty screaming roar
We're forced to drag ourselves back up again
And reinforce our very core
From crumbling down
When we had sunk so low
So low
Upon our quaking knees
So drained of comfort and belief
So weary of this trodden
Beaten ground
That shook beneath our aching feet.

But
Life
Exists
To reignite
The challenge
Of that divine fight
That lies within
Each one of us –
The truth is there inside of us.

And life provides the path
And means
To far exceed
Our sweetest dreams...

And life
Has rainbows waiting there
If we just
Stop

To feel and care
And let
Belief
Transport us there...

And stay a while
And start to smile
And trusting, wait
And just have faith.

This life
Has borne me many tears
Of grief and sadness
Through the years
And fear and pain
And hurt and rage
And feeling trapped
Within this cage...

But life
Has given
So much joy
And love and light
And laughter too
And miracles
And sunshine days
Moments that took my breath away.

And Love –
The greatest gift of all
Allowed my soul to strong stand tall
Allowed my mind
To waive her woes
And put the wiggle
Back into my toes.

This love I've found
Exists in light
That will succeed
The blackest night
And vast exceeds
Our wildest dreams
And drives our very lives, it seems.

The light I found
Whilst crouching low
She at my darkest moment showed
She pulled me up
To start again
Forget about past fears and pain.

And as the light
I welcomed in
I felt my soul
Begin to breathe again.

I learned that we
Are not alone.
I write this song
To pass that on.

## THE MAGIC WITHIN US

We were all born
With great power within us
The magic that makes us
Unique dreams that drive us
As flower buds thirsty
To suck from life's nectar
Delicate
Tender
Resilient
Amazing
Gracing the world
With earnest hope
And pure joy.
Born from a seed
Ignited by passion
Unique, oblique, profound, obtuse
Profusely vulnerable and strong
With our place to belong
Yet no limits.
Naked and innocent
Free and Heaven sent
Here to shine
To be proudly, uniquely us
Emit our magic radiance
And stretch towards the warming sun
To be complete as only one
To glow
To know
Our worth
To show our magic.

## THE NIGHT AFTER CHRISTMAS

'Twas the night after Christmas
And drunk in my chair
I imagined Saint Nic's
Stealthy step on the stair
As he went round to shove
All that stuff in our stockings
(Must be strong – to be fair,
All those things that we've gotten)
All the new gaming games
And the posh picture frames
The new camera twice
(For the twins to be nice)
Then the dinner –
That cost us two hundred or more
Then the great blinking wreath
For the blinking front door
And the shoes
Then the blues
Cos they weren't the right colour
Yes, she'd much rather choose
Well – next time I won't bother...
Still the telly blares out
Baneful blurb from the box
We all slump here and drool
In our new Christmas socks
What a party we've managed
Yes – the food was all swank.
What a shame
That next week
We'll be meeting
The bank.

OLIVE
BRANCH

## THE OLIVE BRANCH

Let's meet at The Olive Branch
Where we can sit
And glance
And gaze into each other's eyes
And be delighted and amazed
As we find
Our human kind
In the meeting of our open minds –
You know that always happens
When we meet
At The Olive Branch.

Let's go to
The Olive Branch
We've not forgotten
How to dance
And sing
And let our spirits ring
Their bells of joy and love-filled things
So we can dance
And twirl around
The ground
As light shines all around
And love and laughter softly sounds
And peace and harmony abounds –
You know that always happens
When we meet
At The Olive Branch.

Let's meet at The Olive Branch
It's always warming for our souls
To wash away our cares of old
And rediscover pots of gold
Just waiting 'neath the sun and rain
Framed by droplets, warmed with rays
As coloured archways guide the way
To beckon in a brand new day
And shed the tears of past time pain
Regather
And regain belief
You know - there's magic in that leaf
You know – we always sort things out
When we meet
At The Olive Branch.

## THE ONE

As I wait for you
I glow
Because I know
You are the one.
When I met you
The sun shone
Back into my life again.
With you I belong.
You are my friend
You are my love
An angel sent
From skies above
To hold me now
Stand by my side
In harmony.
You are the other
Half of me.
You are the soul
Who sets mine free.
With you I always
Will believe.

You understand me
Like no other
Human can
Or ever did
You comprehend me
Without speaking
As we breathe
Sweet words unsaid.
You are my heaven
You are my earth
You are my stars and skies and sun
You are my seas
You are my mountain tops
You are my only one.

It is a choice
We make in life
To share our life
With another one.
You are the one
Whom I have found
To keep my feet
Upon the ground
And raise my soul
Above the clouds.
You make me glow
You make me proud.

It must be fate
That made us two
Cross paths in time
For I am yours
And you are mine,
Our lives entwined.
For you I waited
And would wait still
Yes I would wait
For you until
Life was no more.
The door to peace
Rests at our feet
The door to life
Within our grasp
I couldn't ask
To have one better
Or find another
For you are He
You are my one
The only one
Since time began
That e'er could be
You set me free
You are the only
One for me.

## THE OTHER SIDE

How do I get
From here
To over there?
With that vast swampy, sandy, windy, bendy
Forest beach sea
So snuggled nestling, resting
In between the scenes
Of you and me?
I can see your shores
And hear your beckoning –
Your silent reckoning
On the chances
Of my advances...

Should I take a step?
I might get wet
Or my high hopes dry up.
What if the onslaught
Of the coming tide
Engulfs me as I try to stride?
What if the weird wild wispy wind
Knocks me off my too tired feet
Before I get the chance to meet
Your sweetly smiling gracious
Waiting face?

It's just – this place on which I stand
Renders the shaking of my hand...
I must speak out
And venture out
Before the candle
Of my dreams flickers out.

That bush of thorns,
Though tiny
Still scorns my ache to fly
But I
Will not unto its wily whisper listen;
As long as your sparkling shores still glisten
I will embark upon my mission
To try
To reach your side.

I will decide
To onward stride
Towards the light
Of the other side.

Now – worry done
My life begun
I will walk forwards –
Here I come.

## THE PATH

I've walked alone through golden fields
Those wandering days I need to feel
And sun has shone on yellow yields
As lone I travelled on my path
Of celandines and buttercups
Whose coloured perfumes raised me up
As in they leaned to kiss my feet
Swaying in a breeze so sweet
Projecting loving yellow light
Glowing golden, sunshine light
Caressingly within their grasp
Meandering along my path.

That path I've trod in pouring rain
Though grey surroundings seemed the same
I reminisced of yellow beds
And exercised a new refrain;
As raindrops pelted on my head
And pounded down from looming skies
I took a breath and realised
Regardless what the clouds throw down
No matter if it's sun or rain
No matter how the weather vane
Or if the skies are gold or grey
I'll still walk forwards head held high
And look my future in the eye
My soul, my heart, my name remains
The path is mine and I'm the same.

## THE RAINBOW

I woke up fresh
Though feeling shy
And peered through curtains
At the sky
It lay before me
Grey stroke white
I closed them back
And wondered why.

I went down stairs
To filter out
The sleep
That keeps
The sunshine out
And as I sipped
I fantasized
Through golden filters
In my mind…

I wondered why
I'd felt alone
And felt my life
Was not my own…
I urged myself
To make a start
And from the sad old ways depart.
I knew the answers somewhere lay
Deep hidden in my inner heart.

I knew we'd had
A tough old month
To top off what a testing year
And shared so many sleepless nights
And shed so many worried tears,
But knew those days were over now
And knew that challenge made us grow.

I went into the living room
And stopped
To light a lamp or two
But still the white
Pervaded through
The clear blue crystal skies I knew.

Then as I thanked
For lush green grass
I walked up to the glass
And gasped!

The strangest sight
My eyes did meet…
A rainbow landed
At my feet!

## THE RED ROAR AND GOLDEN HILLS OF WALES

I hear a whisper
Rising
From the steaming golden hills
And mystic mauved valleys
Of the land of the dragons.
A rumour
Floating
Like a wisp on a breeze
Or a feather on a trickle
Of a stream gleaming
Ebbing through the hillsides.

Hear the quiet voices singing
Like the ghosts of gloried past times
Raising rousing from the deep mines
Waking spirits of the old times
From the secret hidden caverns
And beneath the black rock mountains
Comes the lilting of the spirits
Of the waiting, resting dragons.

From within the golden forests
Sounds the singing of the people
Growing louder with each daybreak
Strong pure voices of the humble
And their passion sends a rumble
Through the mountaintops and valleys
Waking Princes and their treasures
Raising giants from the ethers
As they celebrate the dawning
Of a passionate new era.

Feel the echoes on the beaches
That resound around the sand dunes
Belting out the cries of dragons
And the songs of mighty shepherds
Filling skies with fires of scarlet
Filling fields with golden trumpets
And the people lining pulpits
Of their mighty castle turrets
Raise their voices even higher
As the Ddraig ignites its fire.

I am deafened by the daybreak
As majestic male voice choirs make
The mighty moving mountains shake
And sweetly singing women
Hark the wonderful beginning
Of a golden dawn
To softly spawn
A brand new day
To pave the way
That we can say
We rose through pain
To fight through fires
And roar again.

TAILOR
D.THOMAS.
OUTFITTER

## THE TAILOR'S SONG

If you be
Somewhat shorter, Sir
A little larger, Lady
We care not a stitch
Although of course I must declare
Great care goes into every stitch
It's just for us the pull
The itch
To define your wondrous line;
We weren't born of
Production line, human kind
Conveyor belt
Moulds will melt
Some aren't so svelte...
But you can rest at ease
Kind Sir, Madam, please
We don't admire perfection here
Your human form is the allure
Our challenge
My dear, it's why we're here!
We have the knack
And can provide
The shirt for your back
Thin or wide
Tall or short
Tight or slack
We only ask
You wear with pride.

## THE TREE SURGEON

Topographeric trapeze artist
Gravity defies
Topiary in motion framed by tranquil topaz skies
He lives with birdsong day by day
Clouds drift apart to light his way
They dance on by, reflected in his clear topaz eyes.

He flies through branches
Lifts and dances
Works and watches
Never flinches
Cares for wounded souls and soldiers
Loves the same the oaks and alders.

Birds watch over him in turns
Unspoken understanding burns
He sees the world as simply as the charcoal crower flies
Free spirits sharing knowledge crowing empathy belies.

As mortals in grey offices at grey machines comply –
They plod through day, time ebbs away
Their spirits stripped into decay
Unknowing fellow doctors' ways
So never ending, not befriending
Unforgiving, hardly living
Pale and grey they spend the day
Regime that takes their life away
And all the while
Their pallid pinstripes want and weep and sigh…
And every morning in the mirror
Gleaming cufflinks wink and glimmer
They check and wile
A knowing smile
As to themselves they lie.

Still, on the earth,
His free soul works
With Her as one – the lucky one
Upon, between majestic growth
He helps breathe life, induces hope
Our magical tree healer, skyline ballerina flies.

The cold air grips and bites his skin
Yet still he smiles, warmed from within
He looks ahead to beauteous Spring
And to the joyous, loving Summer
When his work is like no other
And warmth and life and leaves unfurl
And abalone reveals her pearl.

Aeons lived, he bares his soul
While he attends, they merge as friends.
Unlike his patients lifetimes old
Who witness epic tales unfold, yet silently
Their tales withhold –
Bestow that duty on their friend –
He is their voice, he sings their songs
For on their earth he too belongs
From mountain tops to ancient sands –
A testament to timeless lands.

And there's no whim to cut his limbs,
Reduce his life by counting rings –
His soul recounts the stories told
Of ages 'riched with pots of gold
All growing in the rich lush ground
And buried at the feet of trees
With bluebells blooming all around
As up above the skylarks sound…
Yes, soaring with them
To the sun
Will always fly
The Tree Surgeon.

## THE WAITING PRINCESS

A Princess sat upon a gate
Waiting for her Prince.
She sat and sighed and rolled her eyes –
That Prince was always late!
But still she loved him
So she stayed
To wait an hour more…
He really was so very kind
She loved his face, she loved his mind
He said he loved her
More than all
The peanuts in Brazil.

She looked again down at her watch
And gasped at what she saw!
Whilst waiting for her handsome Prince
She'd stayed six hours more!!
And still he hadn't shown his face –
Just left her waiting there.
It made the Princess start to think
He didn't really care.
A tiny tear trickled down
The corner of her cheek
And muffled words clogged up her throat
So that she couldn't speak.

But what?
A sound?
Of Prince's steps?
Emerging on the breeze?
She raised her eyes
And Yes! 'Twas true!
She'd raised her eyes to his.
The Princess gleamed
Was overjoyed
Her smile lit up the sun.
Her pain-filled tears vanished
And she glowed because her Prince had come!

He said:
"Hey babe, you're looking swell,
D'ya want to come with me?
I've golden tickets to the ball –
The caviar is free!"

The Princess stopped.

She looked at him.

She thought a little while.

(The Prince began to fidget
At the fading of her smile)

She said:
"You know, I'd love to come
But don't think that I can.
I can't because I don't think
You're my perfect Princely man.
I've waited here
For you, my Love
Seven hours upon this gate.
I think I need
To find a Prince
A little more polite."

B B

## THE WEAKEST LINK

You are the weakest link
My friend
Your quest to think you're
Any more
Ends here.

No – don't implore me
With those doey
Eyes
Not worth the try –
We've cut you right
Back down
To size
And will some more.

Let the people laugh!
It's just a joke!
Let the vultures prod and poke
And rip
Some strips
Of tender flesh
From your heaving
Tender breast.

At my request
They'll hurl you to the ground
And pulp and pound
Your little frame
After all – it's just a game
In the name of fun.

So come on everyone!
What ya waiting for?
What?
You didn't even know
His mother was a whore?
Well, now you know
So have a go!

Dig deep
Into your mean
Reserves
It's no less than
This man
Deserves.

He's lost.
The cost of this
Is shame.
You know – it's just the game.

Let the elephant
Contestants
Shrink –
Become extinct.
These weakest links
Must all be shot.
It's got to be done
For the good
Of the chain
After all – this is the game.

We don't make the rules
You know
We just put on
A dazzling show;
And then,
Good folks,
It's up to you
To do
What you think
Is right to do.

He's fat
She's black
He's young
She's old
She told some really stupid stories
His metal t-shirt's much too gory
She's Welsh
His belt just does not match his shoes...
Which human being will you choose?

They're on a plate...
Decide their fate...
Invoke your strongest powers
Of hate.

It's just a game
It's in the name
And to resist
Would be in vain.

## THERE'S PLENTY MORE FISH IN THE SEA

There's plenty more fish in the sea
You say
But I can't see
Many
If any.

A good fish is hard to find
Simply hard to spot
Amidst
The mired mist
Of winding seaweed gleaming green
Flowing forests who hide the swaying trees
Who in turn hide below their leaves
The life which hides beneath the scene.

And if you do
Spot a good fish
It's just so hard to catch.
It's fighting for survival
And doesn't know who it can trust
Beneath the crusty
Cunning
Overused
Indiscriminate
Abusive murder nets
Of fishing men and women –
Or – their capital commanders...
Who catch them and inspect
If up to scale and scratch
For our all-consuming appetites.

If not
They'll simply toss them back
Doomed to float forever above
The surface of the shining world
That they used to know and love.

What a waste
Of a bazillion unique proud swimming souls
Sacrificed
For a bazillion tubes of fish paste.

We just don't appreciate quality any more.
We destroy the quality
With our quest for quantity
And the quality's left to die off
While we round them all up
And sup
And scoff and stuff our mouths
With the embryonic eggs that house
Their futile, fragile futures.
De-scaled and impaled by our poisoned petards –
God, the life of a good fish is hard.

And all the fish used to be good –
I'm as sure as sushi is salty.
And still are, I'm still sushily sure,
In some remote, advanced localities
Where the culture still understands
The underlying economic landscape
And works and supports to expand
And protect
The swimscope and the swimscape
Of the surviving clans and clams.

Perhaps it's because
All the algae is gone?
That rich fundamental bed of life
Which feeds
All the other life above
With the simple basic necessities
Of nourishment, nurture and love.
And helps the fish to breed and grow –
That creative cushion
Of maternal provision
Resting silently below.
Perhaps it's because that's missing
That we're missing out on all the kissing?

I'm so hungry now...
Really ravenous and feeling slightly weak.
So come on –
Never mind this paltry song –
Let's go my dear and eat.

I think I'll have the Bluefin tuna.

Echo
Centenary

## THIS IS THE TIME

Another time
Another rhyme
Another season
Another treason
Against humanity.

Another time
The same old rhyme
Another season
Another reason
To reach for sanity.

Another day
Another way
The chance anew
A cosmos new
We search for purity.

Same bottom line
Old ancient rhyme
We step in time
It is destined
For all humanity.

Now is the time
Collective minds
And stars align
Our paths entwined
Sublime infinity.

This is the time
The time has come
The stars and sun
All point to one
Divine reality.

## THROUGH THE BOTTOM OF A WHISKY GLASS

Through the bottom of a whisky glass
The grass
Sways most distorted strange
Disseminates
Your golden rays
Engulfs and swallows golden days.

Through the bottom of a whisky glass
I ask
For more untunelled vision
Ask to
Maybe
Halt this indecision
Contemplate the fate of my reprehension
Who waits behind her somber gates
Of judgement
And uninlovement
Yet with her much more lasting covenant
Of gold green gracious sober government.

But yes! I love your golden notes
They float
Through flowered honeyed dewey dreamy
Sleepy
Sleazy
Easy
Unwifeypleasy
Lemon squeezy
Joy
For now, I know.

But is it really you who sways,
Sweet liquid of my anguished days?
Or do the rays
Of sunshine sway?
Or those sweet flowers float away?
Is it the glass?
Or does the leaning grass
Just greenly ask
If my own hand
Or my command
Is the never-ending
Bending
Or the ending of my days?

You take me to a golden place
Though you may lead
To my disgrace…

Through the bottom
Of this whisky glass
Some clarity Is what I ask.

## TIME CHANGES

Time changes
Lends the air
A restless flowing flight
From grounded, steady pace
As soft descends the waking stare
Of aching change on breaking faces
And lines stretch wide
From eye to eye
Their perfect faults run deep
Betraying faltered sleep
As faltering they try to keep
Their step in time
To long-gone, fast-past ancient rhyme
The beat increased
Stepped up
The pressure risen
Rising still the new horizon
Rhythm call
Confounding one and all
As patterns change and break
And planet shakes
Vibrates a new
Time line rhyme running through
And cracks appear
Deeper than before
The ice sheets thaw
And mountains move
And grooves of canyons separate
Like lines dividing love and hate
And dark and light
We wait
We contemplate our fate
Of fight or flight -
The great debate
And through the rainbow
Clouds and thunder
Emanate the restless wonder
As we anticipate the yonder
Time - it changes still.

## TIME SLEEPS

Time sleeps
She waits curled
White all fluffy tailed around
Her body rested sweetly scented mists
Enveloped nestled
Waiting
Sleeping
Conscious waking
Dreaming.
Ready to present to the unbelieving.
She strong conceives
Slow deep steep mountain climbing
Rights of way
And passages
And messages
And messengers
And dawn break and new age old
Waking, waning days
She sways
She bends
Through light and back
To live and breathe
And dance and learn
Retrace the tracks
And set fresh paths.
We grasp her
Fleeting
Longing
Searching
Waiting
Showing
Hiding
Convexing
Confiding.
She passes us by
Stands strong at our side
At our backs
Like the wind
And she flies overhead
Like an eagle
A dove
As below so above
And throughout
She shines through
Within me
And in you
There in us
Deep within
On the cusp
Through the soil
In the soul
Through the starlight glints the gold
Her everlasting rhyme
The night and light divine
Sleep, sweet Time
When you wake
You will be mine.

## TIME STRETCHED

Mystic mists
Of time-stretched twists
And curves
In countless country lanes
The birds sing high
And rainbows fly
Through melted, mauvey
Time-stretched sky.

Then forests loom
And through the green
We drive
Towards
The great unknown

Time edges by
Through dreams we fly
To grow more trees
From seeds we've sewn.

And all the time
The time-stretched rhyme
It fluctuates
Like constant song
The sun will show
At times will go
But on our path
We'll carry on.

## TIME SWEEPS

Time, she sweeps
She runs in blasts like shards
Like swords
Of moments
Space or
God bestows
Bestowed
To give
And give again
A cycle, certain, sure
Aflame
Each day anew to strike
Alight our way
With lessons
Burning
Mother Nature churning
Time glowing
Spinning
Sitting
Showing
Flowing.
Continue, her – as written in her stars
And ours
And in the lines between
Those paving lines of life
We dread to stride
For fear to strike
Our shining mark.
Perspective shimmers.
She begs our silent reckoning
In the hour or moment of our divine reflecting.
Straight, Time stands intent
Yet still she bends and flows
As sharp as clouds and candyfloss
As harmless as the stems of roses
Sweetly hurls the muse she saw or felt or heard
And then by grace composes.
Fireworks oh so calm so soft
She blows by mighty steadfast hand
Then stands strong at our side
Even whilst her will of hell for us she wields.
So, why? Is it her will?
Or is she, like us, a messenger
For a force that's stronger still?

## TO LEARN TO FLY

To learn to fly
Is to experience pain
And suffering
And challenges
And obstacles
Heartache
Worry
Loss
Disappointment
Disillusionment
Disaster!
Exasperation
Jilted imagination
Jolted expectation.

All of these things
Aren't the cruelty of creation.
They're the kindness
They're the gift
They're the essentials
That lift
Our consciousness
And magically move us to express
Our inner feelings.
They're the tools that help us
Keep breaking through those ceilings!

All of this
Is just sweet life
It's what it takes to be alive.
Well, if we haven't really lived, my friends,
How can we learn to fly?

## TOO GOOD

We've all
Just had it
Too good
For too long.
Must be time
To rewrite
The lyrics
Of the song
And put
All us people
Back down
Where we belong.
We've all
Just had it
Too good
For too long.

Must be time to redress
The balance
Of power.
Must be time
To weaken
Us
Hour
By
Hour.
I can hear
The gong
Of the railroad
We're on.
We've all
Just had it
Too good
For too long.

You know
They don't like it
When us lot
Are strong.
When it's right
For all us lot
For them lot
It's wrong.
Because when
We are weakened
We can't challenge
Their wrongs
And if they're
Never challenged
They can just
Carry on.

We've all
Just had it
Too good
For too long.
WE MUST PAY
FOR THE GOOD TIMES
(Like it's us
That did wrong)
And the ones
Who control us
Laugh
As we limp on.
We all
Just had it
Too good
For
Too
Long.

## TOO SAD

We've all
Just had it
Too sad for too long.
Must be time
To rewrite
The lyrics of the song.
And bring all us people
Back up
Where we belong!
We've all just had it
Too sad for too long!

Must be time
To redress
The balance of power
Must be time
To strengthen
Us
Hour by hour.
I can hear the ring
Of the bells as they sing
Must be time
To find sunshine
Outside
And within!

We are all
Just a sunbeam
Here to shine
On this land
We are all
Given answers
Simply waiting
To be found.
We are all God's sweet children
Humbly waiting
To be crowned.
I rejoice
At the beauty
Of the truth I have found
And I laugh
As my heart
Starts to sing
With the sound.

It is Love
That will keep us
Together
As one.
It is Love
That will help us
Keep singing
Our song.
Only Love
Can empower us
To be gentle
And strong
And Love
Who reminds us
We are never alone.

## TWO STEPS

Times.
These times
Confuse the mind.
Take two steps forwards
One step back.
This simple song
Sent to remind
That child -
You're still on track.

TŶ HYLL
Eryri
THE UGLY HOUSE

## UGLY

Ugly is as ugly says
And ugly is as ugly does.

Ugly is a funny word
One of the ugliest words I've heard
One of the words I'd rather not hear
One of the concepts I'd challenge, my dear.

What is ugly?
Who can say?
As the gleaming waters play
As they shine a silver mirror
As we peer, reflection glimmers.

Who decides
Where ugly resides?
Who decides
What ugly makes?

I'd suggest
This word ingests
And incarnates
In those who hate.

Who are we
To judge a face?
Who are we
To scorn a form?

Who are we
To use a word
To evoke pain
In those who hear?

I'd suggest
To take a rest
From hating on
The other one…

I think it's best
To look inside
Examine where
This hate resides…

Because each time
We use that word
To inflict pain
Upon this world…

There is a chance that as we use it
We're the ones who then become it.

For once it's said
And we've had our fun
The damage done
No turning back
We've just become
An ugly pot
Calling a weeping kettle black.

## UNCONDITIONAL LOVE

Unconditional love
Is what I have to do
Is what I have to show
Is what I newly know.

As the power grows and finds itself within
So the nurture shows and love binds love with kin
And as the wheels turn round
And all folks stretch to see
I gain a new love found and my new love found finds me.

## UPON SOME DEEP REFLECTION

I tried to help
Or thought I did
But perhaps
I didn't really try
Was I
Just being
A martyr after all
Crying out
A pathetic call
For attention
To make them feel sorry for me
So that I could absolve
And relieve
The guilt
Of what I did
Or rather
Didn't do
To help
Improve
The situation?

It didn't feel like my intention
At the time.
But that cross
And those thoughts
Are mine
To bear
Upon some deep reflection.

Yes perhaps I really always knew
I wasn't really trying
And probably that's the saddest truth
Behind the tears I was crying.
A great friend of mine
Once said:
"If you're not part of the solution
You're part of the problem."
Well, he's right
I don't suppose, I know –
Deep down I've always really known.

So there's only one path
To take
From now –
After honesty
And deep reflection
And that's the choice
To learn
And grow
And never again
To hide away
From the truth
I really know.

## UPON THE FUTURE TRAIN

Upon the Future Train I sat
In my long stripy dress
And my bright orange hat...
That dress, to impress,
Looked a bit like Chanel
But had born the sweet price
Of one slightly less swell.
I waited and wondered
And looked to the sea
To see dancing on waves
Gleaming image of me...
In the window a figure
Surrounded by light
Reflecting that dawn
Each day will succeed night.
And I swore, one time more
As I looked to the door
I would stride to that sun –
Yes, with confidence run
To my fate
As it waited
We all anticipated
(My journey belated
And by chance rearranged)
It was strange...
As I smiled...
I had known all the while
That the answers were waiting
And they soon would be mine.

## US

When you appeared
My life began to feel complete.
The whole world
Cosmos
Mystery of it
Lay before my feet
Set to unwind.
How did we find us
Each, the other?
Find our one true lover waiting
Contemplating each, the other
Though we did not even know
Until the day our other showed.
How we glowed
Before each other
How love set us
Each on fire
Set to burn
So many lifetimes
Set to shine
Entwine our lifelines.
How we knew!
How did we know?
Yet we knew –
We always did
And how it showed!
We shone together
Two stars shining
Fires combining
Each the other one defining
Each the other's life affirming
Each the other's just deserving
Each, each one's sweet dream fulfilling
Each one's firework, shining, spinning
Merging light and coloured auras
Glinting rays of what could be
Would be
Should be
And is as was
And will be surely
Just as is.
Us
We each the other's ending
Start, beginning, middle, journey
Route and reason
Rhyme and season
Each the one
Each one believes in
Each one's life
The other living
Each one's sins
Each one forgiving
We were born to be together
Born to tread this path together
You and I
Soulmates and lovers
Born to share
This life forever.

## VELOCITY

Velocity
Velocity
Divine reciprocity
Of the urging of the rivers
Crying out to join them
In their tantric flow
They merge combine electrifying
Joining, running, deeply stunning
Perfect shining
Grace entwining
As the lines of two
Seeming divided
Stifled
Free now flowing
Source by source from trace
Eternal one source
Rush the river
Call the dawn of tides within
Her, him
Begin to shine and smile and
Sing through currents
Be one as it takes you
Moves with you to deep calm knowing
Guides you through to deeper waters glowing
Loving
Soft enduring
Warm embracing
Ice fire racing
Guide her song from source together
Rush this calm eternal river
Rush with thunder
Peace beyond her
Through her melting deep
Each drop
Eternal
Not destined to stop
But flow as one almighty rushing
Resting
Urging
Peace-filled
Purging
As she flows toward the tender
As the sunlight glistens yonder
As the storm clouds cease to thunder
As the river merges on
She finds a pool that glistens long
And as she longs
Accepts and joins
Then
River
Pool
All else
Are
One.

## VENUS RISES

Turquoise waters swirl and shimmer
Full, they swell, as hearts of men
Soft beneath the stars there glimmers
Movement from her gleaming turquoise den
Then, a crest of foam appears
Riding on a gleaming turquoise wave
Foam, like cloud-dust, floats and quivers,
Dances as the waiting waters shiver.
Only sound of lark appears now,
Sends her notes like kisses on the breeze
Flies above the swirling whirlpool,
Beckons time to set the Goddess free.
Then, a roar is heard from mountains,
Palm trees shake the wind within their leaves
Bursts appear through cracks like fountains
Raise the skies as universe it breathes.
Breaks, the foam, at magic moment
Birds stand still and hold their song
Flowers strain their necks to witness,
Rivers calm and lovers start to long.
Rises, she, the mighty Goddess
Soft emerges, teardrop new
Flowing tresses fall o'er shoulders
Cascade down her naked body true

As the stars begin to sparkle
Goddess opens eyes that shine
Licks her lips, reborn of passion
Breathes and feels and starts to smile.
Oh! Her breasts!
They promise lifetimes
Arms to hold her babes and loves
Hands to touch, bestow their lifelines
Blessed by Father Zeus on clouds above.
Silent she, yet loud as thunder
Sweet she stands and soft as feathers
Thighs, those thighs, the strides of women
Strong as love, as revolution.
Knowing now, the Goddess stands
As waves and hair dance round her ankles
Stomach fills and Goddess understands
Broken free from karmic shackles.
Born as love, a star to nurture
Born to love, as Mother Nature
Born to give, to each and other
Risen, Venus, star-sent lover.

## WAITING SONG

I watch the busy clouds drift by.
Like charms from far off worlds in space
They seem to fly.
The fleeting promise they represent
Is strange, but lovely in this barren place.

Gone now, and green stench surrounds me.
Decaying Summer grass and leaves
Have found me.
Their sweetness hurts my eyes
And their scent the odious wind upon me breathes.

Shedding bluey shades the sky turns red,
Displays an evil, deadly lure.
Night looms up ahead.
Behind a rock I cry and cower –
How much torture can, must I endure?

Waiting for the sun to appear
Is lonely, is an arduous task
I fear.
And all the sense I can derive
Is but a morsel of the universe I ask.

The dawn behind the hills awaits.
Whilst crouching low, my death
She contemplates
And teasing, a ray she shows,
Then suffocates me with her humid breath.

## WALK ON

Walk on.
Walk on.
Though your spirit be weary and tired.
Though you've carried the weight
Of your past all these years
Now it's time to release
All that guilt, shame and fear
It is not needed now
It is not needed here.
So just let it go...
Let it flow...
Like a bundle on the river
Watch it float, watch it flow
And you'll carry on along your way
Lighter less the load.

Walk on.
Walk on.
Though your spirit be daunted
By what lies ahead
Though you doubt and are frightened by
Words that are said
Now it's time to become
Who you always have been
Time to open your heart
And to raise up your head.
So just let them go...
Let them flow...
All those doubts and the fears
Down that river they go
And you'll carry on along your path
Lighter less the load.

Walk on.
Walk on.
It is time to enjoy now the path that is yours
It is time to appreciate all that occurs
It is time now to celebrate
Time to give thanks.
And as Spirit grows
From within your soul
And divine you glow
As your light unfolds
Darling, let it flow
And that light will show
As along you go
Yes - your soul will show.

## WANTING TO GET ON

Wanting to get on
We swim around
Searching deep
Into the lost and found.

Then search our souls
For there we find
All answers
To the questions
That were muddled by our mind.

## WARRIOR WOMAN

Warrior Woman
Soft, so soft
Your eyes convey a million tears
Burned down oh so tender cheeks
The sacrifice of the almighty meek
The strong, the walking Goddess
In her hips the thrust of mountains.

Warrior Woman
Strong, so strong
Your soul conveys a passion fired
O'er ages, aeons, billowed wild your hair
It glows alight with tales unshared
Your cares and struggles merging
Into sky the clouds are raging
In your heaving, feeling breathing.

Warrior Woman
Warm, so hot
Your passion steams the sky to thunder
Restless in your beauty, tender
Bold compassion, resolution
Stirs the stars to sparkling wonder
Shakes the waking, aching ethers
Hot, you burn like red coal fires
Warm, the coals, your heart's desires.

Warrior woman
Be at peace
Your time has come to rise anew
The arrow set to shoot straight through
The truth it waits, it gleams like sunrise
Set to light the fire in your eyes
Melt into the gold horizon
Raise your arms in tender passion
Love awaits
For earth
And nation
Take your place
Sweet Warrior Woman.

## WE

We
Are all we
And have been since time began
And will be until time ends.

We just have to realise
That we're all
Really friends.

And the syncopated rhythms of our hearts
Beat
To the same simple
Complex song.

We just must distribute the words
So that together
We can sing along.

And I
Will always be I
Despite the tries
To drum me out of me.

And we
Will always be we
Despite the lies
To divide and deceive
Our common mind.
Are we that blind?
They think we are.
And they don't care
About us.

They try to sow
A field of weakened we's
Growing from our lonely knees
A vast expanse across all lands
If divided, we are falling
Then together, we must stand.

It feels
That we are lost
And have forgotten the mortal cost
Of isolation
Within this divided world
And nation.

## WE COULD GET MARRIED

We could get married in a place like this
And right before the archway stand
As we exchange our vows and kiss
And don our gleaming wedding bands;
We'd fill the room with rows of chairs
To seat our family and friends
And feel the glow of warmth and love
Within the walls and up above
We'll have hosts of candles burning bright
Floating soft scent in the air
Dancing shapes on every wall
Flickering their amber light
In this ethereal hall
Glowing, warming one and all
Warming us in our hall;
And flowers standing in great urns
Bending heads towards us two
As we wait to take our turns
To say the sacred words 'I do'.
Yellow, red with white and green
Will proudly decorate the scene
And also lend their giddy scent
Of mellow perfumes heaven sent
To envelop every guest
As peace upon the couple rests.
And as the congregation smiles
We hold hands all the while
And as the congregation sings
They will breathe the incense in
And raise the sky with songs they sing
Words of love, and songs of praise
To celebrate our future days.
As they witness our joy
Of promises that never end
All we need now is us two
Soulmates, lovers and best friends.

## WE'LL ALWAYS BE TOGETHER

We'll always be together
Floating over clouds
We'll always be together
Drifting through soft stars and sky
The we, the us, the you and I
The reasons why this universe
Feels soft, so soft and sweet aglow
With kindred souls like you who know
The we, our heartbeat long entwined
Enshrined together since the dawn of time
The song destined to play eternal
'Cross the wondrous sands of space
To bless us with her holy grace
That when we look into each other's faces
Eyes and smiles, our hearts wide open
Souls exchanging love unspoken
Softly breaks the magnitude
Like dawn upon the golden rocks
As gently as a babe's electric shocks
They ripple through us as the feeling takes us
Grows us, makes us ever stronger
As we sigh and smile in wonder...
So, with fingers touching, minds embracing
Hearts combined and holy heaven racing
Sweet, the beat of just one heart pulsating
We'll always be together
For there's no such thing as parting.

## WHAT ARE WE?

What are we
If not a brief flicker in eternal time?
Or
An eternal flicker
Appearing in the briefest window of space and time?
Or, are we an enduring
Long-burning flame
The imprint of whose essence is infinitely
Stamped in the physical and metaphysical
Consequences of our being and actions
And in the magical residue of that one eternal moment
During the vast expanse of time in which we burned?

Or, do we burn constantly, in ever-evolving
Travelling selves that stretch out our own
Personal time continuum forever across the
Equally infinite universe?

As each death gives rise to continual rebirth
And progress, even at the door of this life's death,
Are we
More strongly and connectedly alive than ever in the
Knowledge that our light will continue to shine?

Can we find others of ourselves? –
Alternative versions of our own current, past and future selves
Co-existing through different vortexes of the universe,
Like separated twins who are inextricably linked
To the other half even though they may have no proof
Or definitive knowledge of their other half's existence?
The feeling is always there…

Whatever, whoever, however we are,
We can surely only exist to be ourselves.
It is the only way that we can justify our existence,
Appreciate it
Give thanks for it
Love the life that is ours
And fulfill our destiny as souls.

We walk alone
And together
For a lifetime, many lifetimes
And mere flickers of time.
We are time.
We are light through space and time.
We are graced
With this hour, this moment,
This lifetime, truth, this flame
Of our infinite
Endless
Glowing
Shining
Beautiful
Burning
Amazing
Inspiring
Journey.

## WHAT IS HEAVEN?

Some want money
Some want power
Some want status
Some want flowers
Some want sex
And some want fame
Some just want
To win the game...

But all of us
From every region
Whatever our personal
Rhyme or reason
Whenever the time
And through every season
We're all just searching
For our version
Of Heaven.

## WHAT IS IT?

What is it that makes our conscious mind
Deviate from truths we hold inside
And render tinted glasses blind
As roses wilt into decline
And lurch the joyous singing child
From innocence to tainted wild
Despair, abandon, sick to find
Unnatural as Lady Scot
Of the play we must not mention...
Did she choose her fated lot –
Abhorrent human foul intention?
Is it the eternal doubt
We learn when life
Our fire puts out –
Denies our optimistic light
From shining through our darkest night?
Experience – it cuts to bear
Then in love's place
A stone sits there
And on love's face
A stony glare
And from without
The silent witness
Cannot comprehend our sickness
Because the world is unaware
How much
And why
Our pain lies there.

## WHAT IS THIS LIFE FOR?

What is this life for
If not to house passion?

What is this life for
If not to take action?

Why have hopes and dreams
Not to gain satisfaction?

What is this life for
If not love
And completion?

## WHAT IT IS

What it is
Right,
Is that
I'm just trying to get along
Trying to sing
A merry song
Without no interference
From those things called
People
And
Life.
Oh – Wouldn't that be nice?
But then again
Through my mists of confusion
I somehow sense
That through this perfect solution
It would somehow be
Quite sad
And lonely
To be all by myself
For this great journey.

## WHEN ALL OUTSIDE BREAKS AND CRUMBLES

When all outside breaks and crumbles
As it does, and as it will
And your heart
Feels heavy with the weighted vision
Of it all - look within.
Deeper than the outside peeling
Paintwork artwork proud facade
That guards who knows but you
What heart it guards - but it is yours.
Deeper than the whitewash touch-up
Fencing round-up spirit kept
Who hides inside their shaking shell
And hides their birthright light as well -
To take that chance!
To lose the coating -
Find the joys of life afloating
Formless, priceless gifts appearing
Manifest in simple treasures
Glowing through the endless ethers
As the shining sunlight sparkles
As the songbird takes to wing
As the sound of love begins to sing...
When all outside breaks and crumbles
Child, just look within.

DADDY

## WHEN EVERYTHING IS NOTHING

When everything is everything
We seek, we try
We search to find
A reason to placate our minds
To fill the space
And cram the void
With everything we should avoid
We break a nail and get annoyed
When everything is everything.

When everything is nothing
We can see the world stripped bare
When everything is nothing
Our first foot stands upon the stair
When everything is nothing
Everything's important
Because when everything is nothing
The matrix world lies dormant.

When everything is nothing
The shoppers pass us on the street
With laden bags and heavy feet
And soul light missing from their eyes
And spoiled, their children pout and cry
They plod on home to open toys
And miss out what their souls enjoy
And make a great almighty noise
But those with nothing – peace.

When everything is nothing
The diamonds still glimmer
Although these precious gemstones lie
Within our eyes – they twink and glimmer
And diamonds on the skinny fingers
Of slender ladies missing dinners
Because they search for affirmation
Comparing waistlines with the nation
And credit cards drive out the bards
Who would enrich their souls and kiss
Their empty eyes and empty cries
And strip away material lies –
Yet when everything is nothing
We're left with what's important.

When everything is nothing
Our soul speaks louder than our clothes
When everything is nothing
We seek to fix our heart – not nose
When everything is nothing
We own the real deal
When everything is nothing
We live, we breathe, we think and feel
When everything we have is nowt
It turns the matrix inside out
Then we're the ones who really know
What love and life and truth's about.

When everything is nothing
The world is stripped to truth.
When everything is nothing
We have the power to see who's who
We have the power
To shower love
Untainted as the stars above
We have the choice
To use our voice
To speak of what's important.

When everything is nothing
We can see the world through different eyes
When everything is nothing
We lose the cloak of thin disguise
When everything is nothing
Not stocks, nor shares, but souls will rise
When everything is nothing
We're left with what's important.

## WHICH OF THE TWO?

When you close your heart
You choose your mind
And nothing then but questions find
Unanswered leaning on your brain
Multiplying doubt and pain.

But when you open your heart
And forget your head
And think with your insides instead
A funny thing
May well appear –
That your head
And your heart
May be far from near.

But which of the two
Do you listen to?
Well, that's for you
To decide, my dear.

## WHO AM I?

Who am I?
Me I am.
Acting else
Would be a sham.
Me I am
For I am me
Cos being me
Is being free.

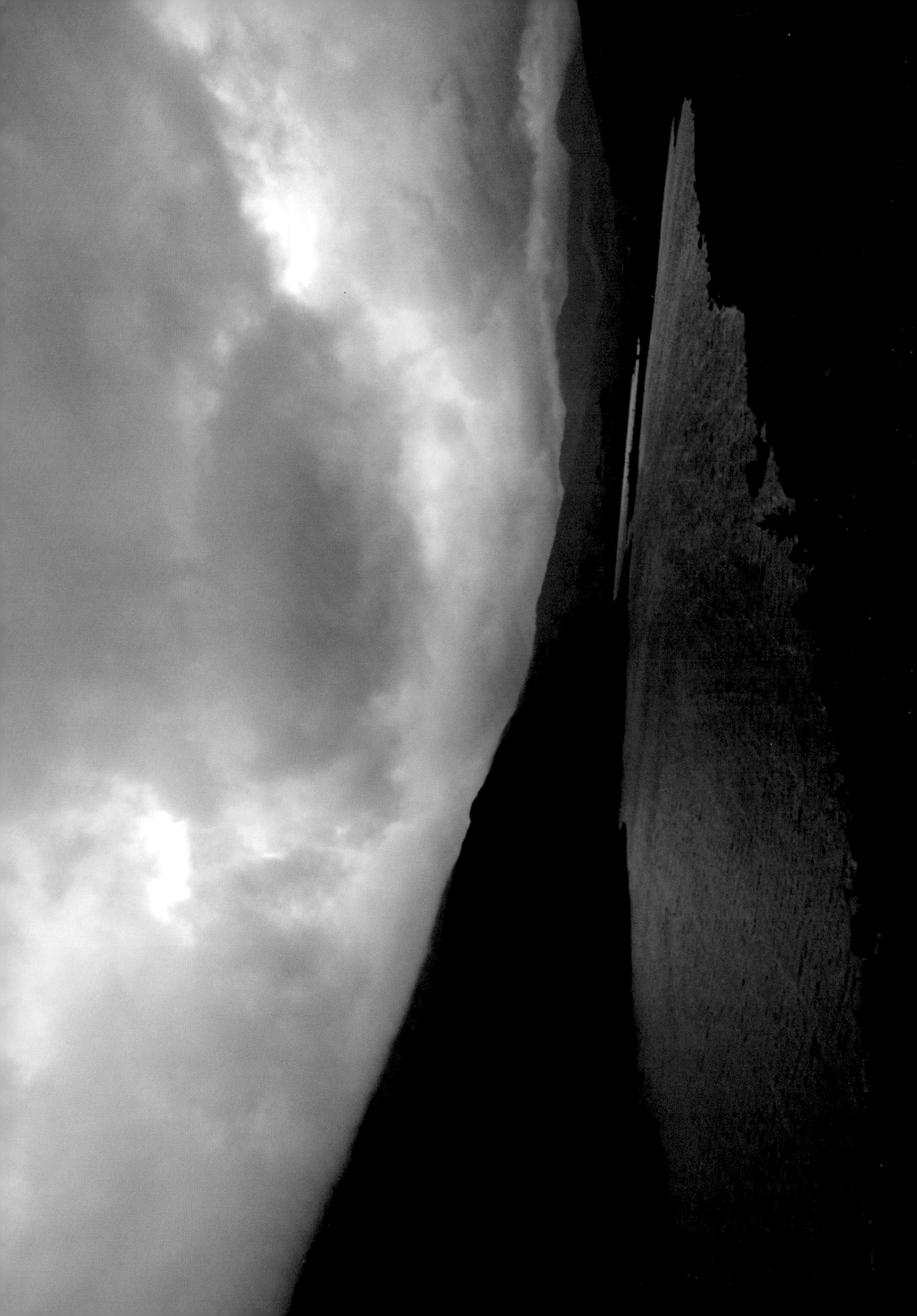

WHY

Why does thunder break
On sunny afternoons just sitting
Dwelling in the love-lit garden
Freely resting, birds a'nesting, singing overhead
And all is wonderful and rosy peachy dreamy
Gazing, leaning with the dreaming flower beds?
Why does it have to break from blue to cold grey rain instead?

Why does it always seem as if
Each time I take a great stride forwards
Seeking out the new and brave - the pathway
Lesser travelled, calling out my soul, my heart, my name...
Whispering – this time will be the time I win the game...
Then once I reach a destination, find it might have been in vain?
Why do I have to start anew to tread the path afresh again?

Why do we ask
Our most profound questions in life
While facing our greatest dilemmas and strife
When things work out wrong or the rain pummels down
When we feel that we never will turn things around
When we're hurt and upset, cold with fears and cares?
Still - we travel on along our sacred route among the stars.

## WORDS

Words words words
The expression of the mind
Giving voice to that behind
The eyes, beguiling smile
Solid, real, defined
A caption for the face
And meaning put in place
For those who are unsure
What feelings hide in there.

Words words words
Of sensual expression
Existential comprehension
Dispelling all confusion
Sourced from sweet discussions
So under no illusions
Reassuring senses
Senses still and rested
Physiognomy complete
With words a face will speak
Of promises devoted
And good intentions coated
In love and adoration
Made real by proclamation
A verbal fabrication
That captures one's emotion
And voice the speaker's passion
To ensure our devotion.

Words words words
On which we build the world
The messages they send
We hear the voice they rend
Words, just words
A tool for fools to hear
Constructed to cast out
Our instinctual doubt
The gift of what we know
Beyond what words will show.

Look again into her face
Peer deep behind his eyes
Though it's tough
Take a breath
And realise
Most words are lies.

## WORSHIP THE WALLS

Worship the walls
That hold you in -
Those sweet containers
For your sin
Protect you from
Your selfish whims
To dance and shout
And fly and sing.

Revere the rules
That rule your days
To keep you from
Your wayward ways -
To laugh and smile
And feel and care
And stride over
The fences there.

Relish the reigns
That reign you in -
You must not to
Your own soul turn
Just fan the flames
Though fires burn
Forget the flight
For which you yearn.

## YOU

You are my universe, you are my star
You are my cosmic gift sent from afar
You are the reason that I'm standing here
You are the one who allows me to care.

You are the sunshine that lights up my sky
You are my treasure, my reason to try
You are the rainbow that shines through my eyes
You are my teacher, you show me the way.

You are my guidance, my soul's shining light
You are the candle that glows through each night
You are my refuge, you are my delight
You are my tenderness, you are my might.

You are the music that moves me to move
You are the melody, you are the groove
You are a symphony singing for love
You are the answer and you are the proof.

You are my oceans, my sparkling seas
You are the wind that love-rustles my trees
You are my dragonfly, king honey bee
You are the love echoes sweet on the breeze.

You are my muse, you are my inspiration
You are my partner within this creation
You are my feeling, you are my emotion
You are my heartbeat and you are my passion.

You are my petal and you are my flower
You are each minute, each lifetime, each hour
You are the magic and you are the power
You are my only one, best friend and lover.

You are my fragrance, the essence of me
You are my freedom and reason I'm free
You are the clear eyes through which I can see
You are the air, you inspire me to breathe.

You are my sustenance, you are my song
You are the one soul with whom I belong
You are the strong one who helps me be strong
You are the one for whom I carry on.

You are the life blood that flows through my veins
You are my reason to push through the pain
You are my thunder and you are my rain
With you, every day I begin life again.

You are my angel, my heaven on earth
You are my laughter, my joy and my mirth
You are the light at the end of the search
You I believe in, in you I have faith.

You are my fairy dust, you are my wings
You are the tune to which my love-bells ring
You are the sweet soul who makes my soul sing
You are my all, you are my everything.

You are my soul mate, my true turtle dove
You are my cosmic mate sent from above
You are my pinnacle, you are enough
You are the meaning of being in love.

## YOU ARE BEAUTIFUL

You are beautiful -
Yes, you.
You're the most beautiful one
That I've ever seen.
Just look at your eyes, how they overflow
With the magic
Of your wondrous soul.
See how they shine
With your lovelight divine
Watch how they twinkle
As the stars
In this great sky;
See how they sparkle
How they dance and set aflame
How they frame
That perfect face of yours -
The face which bears your name;
How they glitter in the sunlight
How they flutter in the moonlight
As a dragonfly, newborn again
Set true to fly through sun and rain,
Reflectors of your joys and pain
The mirrors of your holy grail
The image of your perfect light
Deliverers of your truth inside;
Your gorgeous eyes,
They cannot lie -
Yes, you are beautiful.

## YOU CAN'T GET STRUCK BY LIGHTNING

You can't get struck by lightning
If you don't go out in the rain.
You can't experience pleasure
If you haven't experienced pain.
You can't never lose no losses
If you want to grow and gain.
You can't get struck by lightning
If you don't go out in the rain.

## YOU LIT UP MY LIFE

Whilst wandering in this wondering world
You lit up my life.
When I had thought
That the resting embers of my long lingering hope
Had dwindled into dimness – then I saw you for the very first time.
And a question mark arose to spark a flame.
When I look back – it must have been this way.
I felt a feeling
On that day
The day you noticed me for the very first time –
Or so you say.
The day of the blue top
And my young breasts swelling tight against the wool.
You say they pulled you in.
I like to think my lovely smile
Did some work on you as well.
And once again, when I look back
I think I felt the feeling
Of your eyes awash around me, on me
Felt a tingling, knowing feeling.
Yes - that's the way it must have been.
And then we met.
You - awkward standing with your awkward friends
Unlikely looking Greeks at the front door.
We said a brief hello
Me standing in my devil outfit
And those borrowed knee-high boots.
Completely unaware
Of the effect of the mini skirt and more.
And yet when I look back now
I think I felt you aching
Wondering and searching
Quite compelled by the sweet vision
Of this talking, smiling Goddess
Standing in her devil costume.
And then that night the party.
When we all came back to mine for wine
And you - too shy to speak still
But your thundering presence filling
The whole room.
The gap between us
Must have been at least a metre
And yet it felt like deserts
Stretching out between vast canyons
Climbing mountains, spanning oceans
And yet still It felt like inches
Or an inch
Or maybe less.
I could feel your breath
And hear your heaving heartbeat
In the deafening, roaring silence
Of us chatting, laughing students.
When I look back now to see us
That's the way it must have been.
You spilled red wine
On your best new jumper.
White and fluffy as a cloud from heaven.
Was it
Divine
Intervention?
Was it your subconscious
Romantic intention?
Whatever the cause, the sun and the stars
And gracious fate, arranged a date
And the next hazy sunlit sun kissed day
Your number now stored upon my phone

We arranged for you to come back to mine
To retrieve your white cloud jumper
Sitting soaking in the salt
And to bestow my jumper back –
That you had borrowed in its place.
The knock upon my door
Too early
I fresh from the shower
In a robe
And wet my hair.
You standing there with Tony
And a silly grin.
Was I subconsciously still wearing the robe
To intrigue you or entice you?
I can't imagine that this was so –
It must have been
Divine intervention
Or something else like that.
In any case
Despite your silly boyish grin
I returned to you your jumper
And did not invite you in.
And yes - now when I remember
That's the way it must have been.
And then
That day
That wondrous day
That star shone day
That blessed day
That fated day
In history
In time and space
And destiny
We really spoke
For the very first time.
It was like a clap of thunder.
Like a lightning bolt of rainbows
Hitting soft and seeping flowing
Like a stream
Composed of fairy dust
A river full with magnitude
The energy
Of galaxies
Colliding with a butterfly
Drifting sweet along the breathless breeze
To the harmonies
Of the songs of morning birds
And the swaying whispering chattering
Of the leaves and fairies dancing
To the singing swirling atoms of the awesome timeless wind.
Like a mighty magic oak erupting from the ground
Time sped up twice, a thousand fold the pace
Roots settling deep and stretching far
Beneath the endless Mother Earth
They grew
In minutes
Seconds
Far beyond
Below, above and through
The quaking, awakening horizon
Of the shaking, endless planet.
You told me of your rock.
And I looked deep into your eyes.
Into infinity and beyond.
Down, down, up and through
Into those passageways of light
They led straight to your gorgeous soul
And how it glowed
And called me home.
We played some pool then

And laughed a lot
You in your electric blue jumper that day.
We played
Around the table
Like schoolchildren giggling
In sweet anticipation
Light hearted having fun together.
Then, at one point for some reason
Which I can't remember now
We crossed each others' paths
Skirting, flirting 'round the table
And – somehow from out of the wondrous ethers
Like a magic star shooting through the gleaming soaring sky
I happened upon a chance excuse
Within that briefest second
To kiss you on the cheek.
It was like an electric blue shock.
And time stood still.
We carried on and finished the game
As if the earth moving
Life changing
Soul shaking
Universe making
Kiss on the cheek
Hadn't happened.
But both now grinning, like the cats who got the cream
With spinning stars in our young shining eyes.
And then
We went back to the table
Where our friends were sitting waiting
And we sat next to each other
For the very first time.
With our arms and shoulders touching.
We sat and smiled
And breathed
And held our breath.
With our arms and shoulders touching
Then, our knees began to brush
They rested against each other's knees
They touched beneath the table.
And only us, we knew.
And then
Some minutes, lifetimes later
Somehow
For the very first time
By
Divine intervention
Telepathic comprehension
Existential realisation
Metaphysical manifestation...
Or simply just the miracle
Of everything
In creation...
By mutual complicity
Shining synchronicity
By the grace of God
And time and space
All that ever was and is
And all that ever again will be –
We took each other's hand
For the very first time.
And every planet
Star and moon
In the universe
Began to align.

And that, my darling husband
Is the way it must have been
All those magical moons ago
When us two again began.

## YOUR FUTURE WAITS

Take your leap
Of faith and fate
Fear will keep
Resistance late.
Plunge straight in
The water's clear
You must begin
Your journey here.
Do not cry
Because of fear –
When you try
You'll make it there.
Take the chance
To take your flight
Your soul will soar
When set alight.
Don't hesitate
And don't be shy
Your future waits
To show you why.

## YOU'RE REAL

When I look at you sometimes
I can hardly dare to breathe
Although I know
You're real and breathing
I feel your heartbeat
Pound constantly
Reassuring and lovingly
You fill the room
Without a sound
With presence
Your presence
Love's essence
My love's essence.
Still, after all these years
Of love-filled days
And joy-filled moments
Our treasures uncovered
And to be discovered
You still seem like make believe.
How can I deserve
The look of one so tender
Such deep knowledge and embodiment
Of love's splendour?
My true love and friend
Sent from space or heaven
On a star or ray of sunshine
Blown to me on a timeless breeze
Prophesied by the whispers
Of the dancing trees
One so perfect
How could I have dared
To imagine, or to believe?
Yet here before my eyes
It's true
Stands you
The embodiment of my dreams.

## YOU'VE GOT TO

You've got to
Doubt yourself
To be sure
Of yourself.
This
Is
Your journey.

You've got to
Cut yourself
To find a cure
For yourself.
This
Is
A certainty.

You've got to lose the rest
To find the heart
Of the best.
Painful –
But reality.

You must just impress
The judge of your self.
That
Is
Your destiny.

ZENITH

A dreamy ~ drifting ~ silent haze descends as blanket soft and warm
Blue blanket ~ powder blue it touches ~ soft as misty golden dawn
Caress so soft ~ so tender ~ gentle ~ floats on clouds as dreams o'erhead
Dreams sweet as larksong lilting ~ swaying ~ soars her way o'er flower beds
Enveloping the scene with song ~ her sighing notes they sift along
Faith full for far and future fares ~ they drift their way as whispered song
Grow quiet ~ strong ~ as birdsong hushes ~ silence stills the sacred space
Hugs soft as heaven ~ calm as feathers ~ brushed ~ the blue ~ with winged grace
Imagines true ~ through breath held breeze ~ as wings of bees ~ the silken thread
Joins hands with fairies ~ flitting fireflies ~ glow-worms lighting path ahead;
Kissing trees lean in to meet ~ sweet sapling leaves ~ they laughing mingle
Loving touch ~ their feeling fingers dance as time and space it tingles
Melody fills more the air ~ it swells ~ it blooms as flowerbud glowing
Nightingale peels sweet love's tune as leaves unfurl majestic growing
Opulent ~ rich red as roses ~ scarlet beats the velvet cushion
Passion scented swirling fragrance fills the heart with soft emotion
Quiet breaks the dawn of change ~ its echoes deep as sleeping ocean
Rippling lilting gentle waves ~ they undulate in contemplation
Stars they twinkle in the skies their shining promise of devotion
Time it nods respect ~ it bows to ones here now ~ one inspiration
Universe pulsates with joy ~ as times draw near for evolution
Venus rises ~ shines her lovelight ~ moonbeam firelight revolution
Water rushes ~ fountain flows ~ pure crystal rivers ~ streams run clearer
Xylophones of forests speak ~ the drums they beat as time draws nearer
Yonder o'er the holy mountains ~ angels rise and bells start ringing
Zenith ~ here ~ the path so clear ~ appears the bright new era's dawning

## THANK YOU SO MUCH

The publication of this book was entirely made possible by the support, insight and love of some very special people who chose to help me find Heaven. People who believed in me, believed in themselves, and believed in the power of good that can be accomplished by coming together to help one another.

Sometimes when we simply can't see a way to achieving something, the answer is there all along - staring us in the face in the form of family, friends, and other good people in our lives. Solutions both in the form of our own faith in the existence of these good souls - and of course, in their actual existence - are there all around us every day, even if we don't see or speak to these people every day.

The beauty and miracle of it, is that they do exist, and that the power of love and humanity can overcome anything in our way. When we stop struggling alone and turn to each other - extend our hands to one another in belief, support, and above all, love - anything in the world and even in our wildest dreams, can be achieved.

And in a world with too much want, sometimes the option to be generous is a difficult one to undertake - but those who have ever made that choice will know that not just the external effects of kindness - but also the internal rewards, are far richer than money can buy.

Thank you so much to all of you who have truly generously contributed from the bottom of your heart to support my publication of this collection. You have helped to make my dream come true, and I sincerely wish for you too the fulfilment of your own dreams. You are the ones who inspire me, and you are shining representatives of those souls who inspire good throughout the world. May you always reap the richest rewards in life, and may you always fly strong, high and free. May you find your heaven.

## THANK YOU SO MUCH

My heartfelt thanks go out to: My beloved husband, best friend and soul mate Chrysanthos – my partner in life and in everything I do, whose eternal love, support and understanding has made everything in the world possible. My beloved parents Colin and Lynda Jones – who have been the greatest friends, teachers and supporters a daughter could wish for - and who have give me a lifetime of unconditional love. My amazing friends, mentors and advisers who have been such an integral part of Heaven Is In Here from the outset – Lyndsay Hogg, Jill Gorin, Ed Pereira and Nicola McNeeley. To Gran, Gramps and Nana. To Great-Grandfather O'Hurley. To my beloved parents-in-law Yannis and Nitsa, sister Eleni Vrochidou and brother Alexis Michail. To my wonderful family in Wales and Hellas. To all of my amazing friends in Wales, Hellas and throughout the world - and in particular, to Eleni Sofianou, Annita Tasiopoulou, Angelos Kalogrias, Bobbie-Jo Haarhoff, Andrew and Hajeera DaCruz, Maxine Shervington and Angela Pendegrass. To my wonderful coach Jenny Kovacs of Gift Wish Ltd and inspiring mentors Katharine Dever of Better Morphosis Ltd and Malathy Drew of Whispering Energy. To my inpirational teachers Cerys Preece and Erica Beynon. To all at Watts Gregory LLP. To Mike Johnson at The Coal Exchange, Cardiff; Mike Palmer of Pixelport, Joe Brown and all at Designdough Ltd., Richard and Richard at Pure Emerald. To all at Riverside Farmers Market, Cardiff. To Cardiff Granite Ltd., to T J International Ltd., to Pear Communications Ltd. To all the unknown friends and artists featured in photographs. To everyone who has inspired poetry, photographs, thoughts and feelings along the way. To every special soul who has touched me and others with their love and kindness during this magical journey of ours. To my angels, teachers, guides and healers. To all angels, teachers, guides and healers. To Mother Earth. To God - Great Spirit - Divine Mother. To the Universe. To all the Gods and Goddesses. To every soul who loves.

To you. I thank you from the bottom of my heart.

*Hannah*

## LOCATIONS, DEDICATIONS AND INSPIRATIONS

A Bedtime Song For The Parents And Children Of Caerphilly
Standing on the bridge of Caerphilly Castle, Caerphilly, South Wales, at dusk.

A Bunch Of Daffodils
A farm house on the edge of the forest land near Llyn Clywedog (Clywedog Resevoir) near Llanidloes, in Powys, Mid Wales.

A Christmas Wish With Love
Angel.

A Fleeting Visit To North Wales
Descending the slopes of Mount Snowdon, Snowdonia, North Wales.

A Little Respect
Picnic area at Nestos River, between Kavala and Xanthi, Northern Hellas. This poem was written a couple of years ago for a great friend of mine. Thank you for choosing to start anew my dear. Peace, love and respect to you always.

A Mutual Lesson In Human Interaction
Aberystwyth, West Wales. Featuring my friend from the poem. I do not know your name. I thank you sincerely for our exchange and hope that you are well and happy. I wonder if you will come across these words and your image here. Should you happen upon this humble record of our exchange, please do get in touch. Peace, love and thanks to you.

A Penny From Paul
Behind my parents-in-law's Summer house in Iraklitsa, Kavala, Northern Hellas.

A Valiant Life
The leaning tower at Caerphilly Castle, Caerphilly, South Wales. The poem was written for Gerald, at the Cardiac Rehabilitation Centre in The Princess Of Wales Hospital, Bridgend. It is dedicated to Gerald, my Mother and to You.

All
Lighthouse power generator, St. Anne's Head, Pembrokeshire, West Wales.

Amazing Things
Ladybird in the wildflowers at Cosmeston Lakes, Sully, South Wales.

And They Roared
The Millennium Stadium, Cardiff, South Wales.

Angel
Selenite. For my angels. For all angels. I thank you beyond words.

Another Hat
My beautiful friend Bobbie-Jo Haarhoff and the Magic Hat.

As I Walk
Llansteffan, Carmarthenshire, West Wales. The poem was inspired by Psalm 23 of The King James Bible.

As We Gaze
Gazing out from underneath the Willow trees, Sophia Gardens, Cardiff, South Wales.

At Our Feet
Aberystwyth, West Wales.

Autumn
Autumn leaf in my garden.

Beauty Is Only Skin Deep
Sheep near Llanidloes, Mid Wales.

Belief Lost
Caves at Alistrati, Serres, Northen Hellas.

Believe
Christmas lights in Cardiff, South Wales.

Bend
Amidst the Olive Trees in my parents-in-law's garden, Iraklitsa, Northern Hellas.

Beneath The Snow
Brecon Beacons National Park, South Wales.

## LOCATIONS, DEDICATIONS AND INSPIRATIONS

Blown
My wonderful husband Chrysanthos and on either side of him, our beautiful friends Fotis Deloglou and Eleni Sofianou. This poem was inspired by the title of Blown magazine, published by my great friend Ed. Thank you so much Ed, for all the inspiration, help, belief and support.

Born Free
Cosmeston Lakes, Sully, South Wales.

Bread Of Life
Caroline Gough's Bakery at The National History Museum, St. Fagans, Cardiff, South Wales. This poem was inspired by the image, and by remembrance of days of childhood, queuing up at the local bakers first thing in the morning, chatting with our neighbours as we all stood there together, waiting in line for the steaming fresh batch to emerge hot and ready from the oven.

Cariad
Somewhere between North and Mid Wales.

Celebrating Lilies
Lilies in my garden. This poem was written for my Father. I dedicate this poem to you, Dad, to Nana and Gramps, Gran and Aunty Pam. I love you all so much.

Change
Bala Lake, Gwynedd, North Wales.

Cherish The Old
The poem was inspired by my first meeting with the beautiful Gail Lewis of Conservatory Antiques, at her wonderful space in The Pumping Station, Cardiff, South Wales. The image is my favourite piece of furniture; an antique bookcase made by my Great-Grandfather O'Hurley. Thank you so much Gail. And thank you Great Grandfather, for the years of joy and inspiration. To my great-grandparents, grandparents, parents, guides, teachers, ancestors and elders - thank you so much.

Children Of The World
Maria, Mama Nitsa, Aunty Tula and Aunty Georgia dance together at Agiasma, Kavala, Northern Hellas.

Choices
Carreg Cennen Castle, near Llandeilo, West Wales.

Choose Me
Lamp and light bulb in my living room.

Come Fly With Me
Cosmeston Lakes, Sully, South Wales.

Cruel World
St. John The Baptist's Church, Cardiff, South Wales. The first few lines of the poem were written the day that Michael Jackson passed from this life. The poem was completed a year or more later, by which time it had become a very different poem than I had imagined it would be. To Michael – with so many thanks for your service.

Cwtch Cottage
Cwtch Cottage, a Bed and Breakfast guest house in St. Davids, Pembrokeshire, West Wales. The poem was inspired by the image and name of the house. Cwtch means 'hug' in Welsh.

Cycles
Spring in Sophia Gardens, Cardiff, South Wales.

Dance
My beautiful cousin Clare and her wonderful husband Justin dancing at their wedding. This poem is dedicated to Clare and to my Gran. And to all Grandmothers and their children everywhere.

Dewdrop
Inspired by and written for my Father. Near Capel Curig, Snowdonia, North Wales.

Don't Be A Sheep
Sheep at Brecon Beacons National Park, South Wales.

Drop Your Mask
Shop window in Kavala, Northern Hellas. The poem was inspired by and written for my good friend Ed, who was able to drop his mask and allow our friendship to flourish.
Thank you, my dear.

Dusky Cardiff Streets
Cardiff, South Wales at dusk.

Enjoy!
Driveway leading to The Warpool Court Hotel, St. David's, Pembrokeshire, West Wales.

Every Day
With my wonderful husband Chrysanthos at Cosmeston Lakes, Sully, South Wales. This poem was inspired by and written for all of my beloved family and friends, whom I might not see or speak to every day, yet whom I am with every day, in never-ending love. This poem was written for you. I am with you always.

Faith
Carreg Cennen Castle, Llandeilo, West Wales.

Family
Cosmeston Lakes, Sully, South Wales.

Fat Cat Attack
View of Kavala Castle and port by night, from NOK, Kavala, Northern Hellas.

Fear
Graffiti art on a dedicated graffiti wall in Cardiff, South Wales. Thank you to the unknown Artist, for your awesome artwork. Do get in touch, to be credited for your creations.

Fly
Red Admiral butterfly at The National Botanic Garden of Wales, Carmarthenshire, West Wales.

Forget It
Picnic area in Snowdonia, North Wales. Written in a London railway station at rush hour.

Forget We Not
Forget-me-nots in my garden.

Friend
Strolling through The Sticks in Llansteffan, Carmarthenshire, West Wales. This poem was written after a telephone conversation with my wonderful friend Annita, whom I love and miss very much. Whilst writing the poem, images of all my beautiful friends and family, in Hellas, Wales and all over the planet, kept coming to the surface. This poem is dedicated to Annita and to all my beloved friends and family, whom I may not see or speak to as much as we would like, but who are always in my heart and at my side. You are always in my heart, I am always at your side.

Fruit Seller
Pawel Wisniewski, of Tŷ Mawr Organic Farm, Abergavenny, Monmouthsire, South Wales. At Riverside Farmers Market, on the Fitzhamon Embankment, Cardiff, South Wales. This poem is dedicated to Tŷ Mawr and all at the Riverside Farmers Market, who provide the shopping highlight of my week each Sunday. With many thanks also to Steve Garrett.

Full Circle
Kitchen paper towel. Written for my beautiful friend.

Give A Little Sugar
Coco's restaurant, Antigua.

Go With The Flow
Portmeirion Village, Portmeirion, Snowdonia, North Wales. This poem was written for and is dedicated to my great friend, mentor and advisor Lindsay Hogg. Thank you so much for your guidance, support and inspiration. You truly are a shining star. And to all of us. We are all stars, whose sole purpose is to shine as the amazing beings we are.

Golden Bubbles
Sygun Copper Mine, Beddgelert, Snowdonia, North Wales.

Goldfish Bowl
Trout farm at Kefalari, Drama, Northern Hellas.

Grapefruit
Apples and Lemons.

## LOCATIONS, DEDICATIONS AND INSPIRATIONS

Heaven Is In Here
In my parents-in-law's garden, Iraklitsa, Kavala, Northern Hells. With heartfelt thanks to my beautiful friend Angela Pendegrass, a fellow poet, who inspired the title Heaven Is In Here. Thank you for being such a wonderful friend, angel and inspiration to so many of us.

Her Spirit Speaks
Lotus Flower at The National Botanic Garden of Wales, Carmarthenshire, West Wales. This poem was inspired by the amazing paintings of my talented young cousin Chrysa Gkanoudi and the beautiful sense of serenity and calm she conveys in her artwork. Thank you so much Chrysa, you truly are an amazing talent and inspiration.

Home
St. Fagans National History Museum Of Wales, St. Fagans, Cardiff, South Wales. Inspired by the photograph, this poem was the first written in the collection, and the first I had written for very many years.

Hopes And Dreams
Grasses and wildflowers at Capel Curig, Snowdonia, North Wales.

Humanity
Tree Of Love.

I Am A Soul
In the palace of King Philippos – The father of Alexander The Great. Krinides, Northern Hellas.

I Don't Know Why I Love You But I Do
'The Blackbird Tree', in my garden. The poem was inspired by and written for my guides, angels, teachers, mentors and so many amazing, much loved souls in my life. Thank you so much for your love, support and guidance. Words cannot express my love and gratitude. Maxine – the photograph is for you.

I Feel So Lost
Capel Curig, Snowdonia, North Wales.

I Have A Question
Capel Curig, Snowdonia, North Wales. The poem was written after visiting the beautiful Beth Layne's website and reading her poetry, which you can do at http://bethlayne.com/ Thank you so much Beth.

I Wish I Was A Duck
Ducks at Sophia Gardens, Cardiff, South Wales.

I Write For Peace
Cosmeston Lakes, Sully, South Wales.

If Music Be The Food Of Love
Violin.

Image Is Important
The Nike of Samothraki – also called The Winged Victory of Samothraki – at the Island of Samothraki, Northern Hellas. The original statue is now held at the Louvre. The poem was written during discussions with my friend and mentor, Lindsay Hogg.

Individuality
Cows on the cliff tops of St. Anne's Head, Pembrokeshire, West Wales.

Inspirational
Butterflies and Dragonfly at Cosmeston Lakes, Sully, South Wales.

It's Good To Talk
The waters and cliffs at Barafundle Bay, Pembrokeshire, West Wales. This poem appeared following a conversation with my great friend, mentor and accountant, Lindsay Hogg. It showed me that simply by talking honestly and openly with each other, even an accountant and a poet can make perfect sense of one another!

Join
A couple enjoying the sunset, Cosmeston Lakes, Sully, South Wales. I do not know your names. I did not want to intrude upon your beautiful moment. Please do get in touch should you wish to be known and acknowledged as the couple in this image. The poem was inspired by and is dedicated to my wonderful friend, the fair maiden Bobbie-Jo Haarhoff.

## LOCATIONS, DEDICATIONS AND INSPIRATIONS

Joyful
Cherry Blossom tree.

Keep My Love
View from Coco's, Antigua. This poem is dedicated to Maxine, whose words gave life to the lines 'We cannot choose The way to go The path will show.' Thank you so much for everything. It is so wonderful to have you in my life. Keep my love always in your heart. You are always in mine.

Keeping Going
On the road somewhere in Mid Wales.

Leaders Of Tomorrow Picking Daisies In The Sun
Dog Daisies growing wild in the grounds of St. David's Cathedral, St. David's, Pembrokeshire, West Wales.

Lilac Fairy
Lilac Fairy, by Nikolas Haarhoff. Thank you so much Nikolas, for being such a wonderful soul and inspirational human being to everyone around you. You are the Prince of gentleness, knowledge and understanding. I love you so much and always will. You are always in my heart.

Llansteffan Muses
Scot's Bay, Llansteffan, Carmarthenshire, West Wales.

Lost In May In My Garden
Aquilegias in my garden in May.

Love Is The Greatest Gift
A natural heart shaped grass formation, near Llyn Clywedog, Llanidloes, Mid Wales.

Love, Live And Learn How To Fly
Standing near the peak of Mount Snowdon, Snowdonia, North Wales.

ove Rose
Humanity Rose in my garden.

Love – You Will Survive
A heart on the lake at Porto Lagos, Komotini, Northern Hellas. This poem was written for my darling Theos Takis. I dedicate it to you, Theo; to all my wonderful family and friends in Hellas, and to everyone in the world who loves.

Memory
View from Dolbadarn Castle, Llanberis, Snowdonia, North Wales. This poem was written in 1997

Money Doesn't Matter
My beautiful sister Eleni Vrochidou, walking the path from Carreg Cennin Castle, near Llandeilo, West Wales.

Mother Earth
View from Mount Snowdon, Snowdonia, North Wales. For Mother Earth.

Mum And Dad
My beloved Mother and Father at Iraklitsa, Kavala, Northern Hellas. This poem was inspired by and written for you, Mum and Dad. I love you more than words can say and thank you with all my heart and soul.

Muse
Foxgloves. This poem is dedicated to my Mother, who always encouraged me to reach for the stars and told me that I could do anything I wanted to in life. Mum, you are the most wonderful mother anyone could possibly wish for. Every time I see a lovely Foxglove I think of you. Thank you for your eternal love, guidance and belief and for being such an amazing muse in my life.

My Best Friend's Kitchen
Orb in the beautiful Bobbie-Jo Haarhoff's kitchen. This was written for you Bobbie-Jo, and inspired by us.

My Human Right
Butterfly in a glass.

My Particular Part To Play
White feather, emerald grass.

My Space
Lamp in my living room.

My Sweetest Gift
Through the curtains, through the trees. For all my angels and guides. For Maxine who showed me the way.

## LOCATIONS, DEDICATIONS AND INSPIRATIONS

Mystic Spirit
Full Moon in Beddgelert, Snowdonia, North Wales.

Neighbours
A row of neighbours in St. David's, Pembrokeshire, West Wales.

No
Candle.

Nobody Cares
Spider and the web. The poem was inspired by a conversation with my lovely friend Prakriti, otherwise known as @theevilp on Twitter. Thank you so much Prakriti, for the challenges, discussions and many inspirations. Much love and always caring.

Ode To A Tourist
View from Coco's, Antigua.

Ode To Pelagia
Grasses at Cosmeston Lakes, Sully, Penarth. Inspired by and written for my beautiful friend Pelagia Katsaouni, whom I met whilst flying back to Wales from Hellas. With all my love and thanks Pelagia.

Oh Fairy Fortress
The Millennium Stadium, Cardiff, South Wales.

Oh In The Long Winding Billows Of My Mind
Sygun Copper Mine, Beddgelert, Snowdonia, North Wales. This poem is dedicated to all those souls who worked in this and so many other mines throughout the world - and who still work in the world's mines, deep in the belly of Mother Earth. Thank you so much for your vital contribution. We are ever learning from the lessons we are taught by your heroic work, service and experience.

One August Sunday Morning
August sky above my home, Cardiff, South Wales.

Open
Portmeirion Village, Portmeirion, Snowdonia, North Wales.

Parallel World
Llyn Gwynant, Snowdonia, North Wales.

Peace
Cosmeston Lakes, Sully, South Wales.

Perfect
Speckled Wood Butterfly. The poem was inspired by my wonderful friend, Frankie, whom you can meet at @JustCallMeFrank or at www.justcallmefrank.net Thank you so much Frankie, for being such an inspiration to so many of us. Thank you for being so beautifully you, for shining so brightly and for being absolutely perfect exactly as you are.

Progress
Beddgelert, Snowdonia, North Wales.

Pulse
The palace of King Filippos, Filippi, Northern Hellas.

Quietude
Cosmeston Lakes, Sully, South Wales.

Reincarnation
Giagia Yiannoula in Iraklitsa, Kavala, Northern Hellas.

Rise Up The Gods!
Inside St. David's Cathedral, St. David's, Pembrokeshire, West Wales.

Season's Blessings
Icicle-covered Blueberry bush.

Shine
Inside Picton Castle, Haverfordwest, Pembrokeshire, West Wales.

Shout
Art on a dedicated Graffiti wall, Cardiff, South Wales. Thank you to the unknown artist for your beautiful piece. Please do get in touch to be credited for your work.

Side By Side
Tulips at Roath Park, Cardiff, South Wales.

## LOCATIONS, DEDICATIONS AND INSPIRATIONS

Sing
Model Miner at Brecon, South Wales.

Sleep, Sweet Child
The Fairy in the garden.

Smile
My beautiful sister Eleni and beautiful cousin Maria, in Agiasma, Kavala, Northern Hellas.

Someone
Lighthouse at Roath Park, Cardiff, South Wales.

Sometimes We Can Feel So Small
My wonderful friend Eleni Sofianou, at Caerphilly Castle, Caerphilly, South Wales.

Sssshhhh
Fairy light.

Stand Behind A Waterfall
Standing behind Ystradfellte Waterfalls, Neath Valley, South Wales.

Stand Up, Beautiful
A horse at St. Davids, Pembrokeshire, West Wales. This poem was inspired by my beautiful friend Beez Laine, a wonderful human being and poet. You can meet Beez at http://beezknez-beezknez.blogspot.com.au/ or at @Beezknez . Thank you so much for being such an inspiration and for shining so brightly. You are a true queen honey-maker.

Strong
Trees in the park at Penarth, South Wales. This poem was a gift for my wonderful friend Frankie whom you can meet at @JustCallMeFrank or www.justcallmefrank.net, who is one of the strongest people I know. It is also a gift for us all. Strength, love and peace to you always.

Summer Is The Time For Love
Sunflower. This poem was written for my lovely friend Javed. Wishing you a beautiful Summer, this year and every other my dear. To all the lovers out there - may you find the one true love your soul is seeking. May your love be blessed with sunshine and blossom as the finest rose.

Sunshine Mists
Capel Curig, Snowdonia, North Wales.

Survival Of The Fittest
Cosmeston Lakes, Sully, South Wales.

Sweet Bee Fly Free
Bee and Hydrangea.

Synchronicity
Dragonfly and butterflies in the wild grasses at Cosmeston Lakes, Sully, South Wales.

Thank You
Sunshine and flowers in my garden.

Thank You For Being In My Life
Yellow flowers. This poem was written as a continuous tweet poem and inspired by a conversation with my wonderful friend Kerry. For you Kerry and for all my beloved friends and family – Thank you so much for being in my life.

Thank You For Believing
Tulips. This poem was written for some most amazing people in my life who have helped me a great deal in so many ways, perhaps most importantly, by the belief they have shown in me and in Heaven Is In Here. For my wonderful friends and mentors Ed Pereira, Lindsay Hogg, Jill Gorin and Nicola McNeely. It is also for my Mum, Dad and husband Chrysanthos. And for everyone who has ever believed in me. This poem is dedicated to you. Thank you from the bottom of my heart.

Thank You For The Universe
Lilac Flower in Giagia's garden, Agiasma, Northern Hellas.

The Answers Are Blowing In The Wind
Dandelion fairies at Sophia Gardens, Cardiff, South Wales. The poem was inspired by Stevie Wonder's song The Answer Is Blowing In The Wind and contains words inspired by, or spoken by my wonderful friend Maxine Shervington. Thank you both so much. May we all find our answers.

## LOCATIONS, DEDICATIONS AND INSPIRATIONS

The Coal Exchange
Inside The Coal Exchange, Cardiff Bay, Cardiff, South Wales. Today, this beautiful historic building houses concerts, functions, theatre and events. And the old magic energy of the place is still so tangible you can feel it in the air. This poem is dedicated to my wonderful friend Mike Johnson, who tirelessly works so that this glorious building still lives on today - and to the countless miners and mining families in Wales and the world over who have sacrificed so much for their noble cause. Thank you.

The Field
Cosmestion Lakes, Sully, South Wales.

The Gold Across The River
Ogmore-By-Sea, South Wales.

The Key
Standing on Scot's Bay, Llansteffan, Carmarthenshire, West Wales, looking over to Ferryside.

The Light Will Shine Again
Sea front at Porthcawl, South Wales.

The Magic Within Us
Dahlias at The National Botanic Garden of Wales, West Wales.

The Night After Christmas
The real Father Christmas, made out of clay and paint.

The Olive Branch
The Olive Branch restaurant, Aberystwyth, West Wales. Thank you so much for the inspiration.

The One
My gorgeous friend Hajeera, waiting for her wonderful husband Andrew on their wedding day. This poem is dedicated to Hajeera and Andrew. May you live a blissfully happy and healthy life together. Also to my husband – my own special one - who inspired the words as I remembered how I felt as a bride the morning of our wedding. Thank you for being simply perfect in every single way. Thank you for being my one and walking this path with me. I love you more than words can say.

The Other Side
Portmeirion Village, Portmeirion, Snowdonia, North Wales

The Path
Cosmeston Lakes, Sully, South Wales.

The Rainbow
Rainbow in my back garden.

The Red Roar And Golden Hills Of Wales
Standing on Mount Snowdon with friends, looking down at Llanberis Pass, Snowdonia, North Wales.

The Tailor's Song
D. Thomas Tailor and Outfitter at St. Fagans National History Museum Of Wales, Cardiff, South Wales. This image inspired the poem. Thank you so much to all traditional crafts people everywhere.

The Tree Surgeon
Martin Evans of Cardiff Tree Services. This poem was inspired by and is dedicated to our fantastic tree surgeon Martin Evans. To you Martin, and to all other tree and plant healers out there. Thank you so much for looking after our friends the flowers and foliage. Thank you for looking after us and our planet in the process.

The Waiting Princess
The Waiting Princess, by Sophia Haarhoff. Thank you so much Sophia. You are our beautiful Princess of wisdom, love and compassion. Thank you for shining your light so brightly and for your wonderful creative contribution, caring and expression. I love you so much and always will. You are always in my heart.

The Weakest Link
A row of houses in Aberystwyth, West Wales.

There's Plenty More Fish In The Sea
Searching the sea pools at Llansteffan, Carmarthenshire, West Wales.

## LOCATIONS, DEDICATIONS AND INSPIRATIONS

This Is The Time
Clock and Christmas lights in Cardiff city centre, South Wales.

Through The Bottom Of A Whisky Glass
Through The Bottom Of A Whisky Glass

Time Changes
Komotini, Northern Hellas.

Time Sleeps
Cosmeston Lakes, Sully, South Wales.

Time Stretched
In the forest near Llyn Clywedog, Llanidloes, Mid Wales.

Time Sweeps
Kavala, Northern Hellas.

To Learn To Fly
Standing in Llanberis Pass, next to Mount Snowdon, Snowdonia, North Wales.

Too Good
Old buildings in Kavala, Northern Hellas.

Too Sad
The National Botanic Gardens Of Wales, Carmarthenshire, West Wales.

Two Steps
The National Botanic Gardens Of Wales, Carmarthenshire, West Wales.

Ugly
The Ugly House, Snowdonia, North Wales.

Unconditional Love
Angel

Upon Some Deep Reflection
St. Fagans National History Museum Of Wales, Cardiff, South Wales. Thank you so much to my wonderful friend Robert Spencer, whose friendship, love and words of wisdom have been an inspiration for so many years.

Upon The Future Train
Snowdon Mountain Railway, from Mount Snowdon, Snowdonia, North Wales.

Us
With my beloved husband, Chrysanthos, at Porto Lagos, Komotini, Northern Hellas. For my wonderful husband Chrysanthos. Darling, I love you more than words can say. This was inspired by and written for you. It is for you and for us. It is for all the soul mates and ones who are meant to be in each other's lives.

Velocity
Swallow Falls, Betws-Y-Coed, Snowdonia, North Wales. This poem flowed from me like a river whilst listening to an audio gift from the beautiful Katharine Dever, whom you can meet at http://katharinedever.com. Katharine, this poem is dedicated to you. Thank you so much for your amazing work and for being such a great inspiration to myself and so many.

Venus Rises
Turquoise waters of Antigua.

Waiting For The Sun
Alder trees against the sky. Written in 1997.

Walk On
Nestos River, forming a natural border between Kavala and Xanthi, Northern Hellas.

Wanting To Get On
Swan at Cosmeston Lakes, Sully, South Wales.

Warrior Woman
Portmeirion Village, Portmeirion, Snowdonia, North Wales. This poem was inspired by my beautiful friend Soni, an amazing sweet strong warrior woman of our times. You can meet her at @Vidyut or http://aamjanata.com/ .Thank you Soni, for being such an inspiration of strength and beauty to so many of us and for your wonderful contribution.

We
Holding hands with my husband at Cosmeston Lakes, Sully, South Wales.

## LOCATIONS, DEDICATIONS AND INSPIRATIONS

We Could Get Married
Caerphilly Castle, Caerphilly, South Wales.

We'll Always Be Together
Yellow Roses. This poem is dedicated to my friend Davinder Sindhu. It was inspired by his mentioning the song Electric Dreams, by The Human League. For all my friends – for us all.

What Are We?
Candle

What Is Heaven?
Flowers at The National Botanic Garden Of Wales, Carmarthenshire, West Wales.

What Is It?
I wrote this poem inspired by communications with my dear friend Ed. It is also inspired by and dedicated to two of my favourite muses - William Shakespeare and William Blake.

What Is This Life For?
Flowers under the sea.

What It Is
Crab at Scot's Bay, Llansteffan, Carmarthenshire, West Wales.

When All Outside Breaks And Crumbles
Komotini, Northern Hellas.

When Everything Is Nothing
Underneath Penarth Pier, Penarth, South Wales. This poem was inspired by and is dedicated to my beautiful friend @CrankyPappy. To you Pappy and to every other beautiful soul in this world who has everything. Everything in the world is within us. Anything else is nothing.

Which Of The Two
Signpost in Brecon Beacons National Park, South Wales.

Who Am I?
In my parents-in-law's garden, Iraklitsa, Kavala, Northern Hellas.

Why
Capel Curig, Snowdonia, North Wales.

Words
Our great friend Fotis Deloglou and Chrysanthos my husband at Southerndown, South Wales.

Worship The Walls
Harlech Castle, Harlech, North Wales.

You
Chrysanthemums for my Chrysanthos, with all my love and thanks forever.

You Are Beautiful
Swan at Cosmeston Lakes, Sully, South Wales.

You Can't Get Struck By Lightening
Llyn Gwynant, Snowdonia, North Wales.

You Lit Up My Life
Sunset from Thassos Island, Northern Hellas. For my darling husband Chrysanthos, with all my love.

Your Future Waits
View from  Thassos Island, Northern Hellas.

You're Real
My darling husband Chrysanthos, at Capel Curig, Snowdonia, North Wales. For you honey, with all my heart and soul forever.

You've Got To
Llyn Gwynant, Snowdonia, North Wales.

Zenith
Sky, clouds and sunshine rays from North Wales.

For my wonderful parents Colin and Lynda and my amazing husband Chrysanthos. I dedicate this book to you. Thank you more than words can say for your eternal love and support. This book would never have been possible without you. You are my greatest inspirations.